AVIATION
OF BR

Ken Ellis

Midland Publishing Limited

Dedicated to all those organisations – large and small – who are brave enough to open their doors and let their pride and joy go on display to the public.

Published by
Midland Publishing Limited
24 The Hollow, Earl Shilton
Leicester, LE9 7NA, England

ISBN 1 85780 032 X

Design concept and layout
© Midland Publishing Limited and
Stephen Thompson Associates

Printed in England by
Hillman Printers (Frome) Limited
Frome, Somerset, BA11 4RW

Title Page Illustration:
The main aircraft display hall at the Aerospace Museum, Cosford. The upper level walkway affords good views and allows visitors to look right into the cockpit of the Dakota.
(Aerospace Museum)

Cover Illustrations courtesy:
Front, Alan Curry; Rear top, Newark Air Museum; Rear bottom, Fleet Air Arm Museum.

CONTENTS

Acknowledgements

Many thanks go to all of the curators, information officers, volunteers etc who responded to the questionnaire that was sent out fact finding for this book. Thanks also to the museums who helped with illustrations. Other photographs came from many friends around the country and they are credited with their work. The team at Lincoln Graphics sorted out the maps in double quick time. Continued thanks goes to the small army of loyal scribes who contribute regularly to *Wrecks & Relics* – keep at it folks, you get mentioned in despatches in Edition 15! To all the team at Midland and of course to Pam and Fleas.

INTRODUCTION

There has long been a need for a book on aviation museums that works 'harder' than most. Listening to fellow enthusiasts over many years always left me with the feeling there was much more a 'guide' could do for them.

The most important concept addressed here may well be seen as heresy to some — that there is more to life than aircraft! Many an aviation enthusiast is to be found happy as a lamb wending through the locomotives at a steam museum, or vintage car collection or the Victoria & Albert. More than this, there is the family to take into consideration and a visit to an aviation museum can be extended to find something else that will please the rest of the household as well. This book has been devised to offer other alternatives, hopefully not by way of a sop to 'her indoors' but to allow everyone to find venues of interest and, who knows, to make it easier to visit an aviation museum next time!

With the co-operation of the museums concerned, greatly expanded information has been given on the facilities that are available at museums – some that may be quite crucial to a successful family day out. It is believed that *AMB* is the first aviation museum guide ever to provide details of how to travel to these venues by public transport and which offer help to the disabled. Great emphasis has been made of the excellent services to be had from the Tourist Boards, a source all too frequently overlooked by many visitors.

The book has adopted, with a few 'tweaks' the larger 'regions' used by the English Tourist Boards as a more useful way of showing touring possibilities. County boundaries are shown on each of the map 'headers, but readers are reminded that we are all soon to be thrown into turmoil again with the next reshuffle!

Another cornerstone of the book has been to include only museums and collections that are truly open to the public on a regular basis. The general ruling has been only to include venues that are at least open at weekends throughout the summer season. Other venues that genuinely encourage visitors by prior arrangement are given briefer mentions.

The illustrations attempt to show the broad sweep of aviation museums in Britain – there is a wondrous variety out there to sample. Hence there are photographs of displays, as well as airframes for it is often the latter that 'capture' visitors for longer. To add further flavour to the pictorial element some views of exhibits 'in action' before retirement are also included.

The contents of *AMB* have been arrived out from the suggestions of many friends over the years and it is hoped the book adds to the enjoyment of readers as they follow their interests. Comments, suggestions and additions are very welcome so that the next edition will 'work' even harder for you!

Ken Ellis
Barrowden, Rutland
June 1995

HOW TO USE THIS GUIDE

The guide is arranged by large regional area, roughly corresponding to those adopted by the English Tourist Board. Each regional heading includes the counties grouped in that region and telephone and fax number of the Regional Tourist Board(s) (RTB) responsible for the area. General tourist enquires can be handled by the Tourist Information Centre (TIC) number given in the specific museum reference, but more regional enquiries may well be best centred on the RTB.

Museum Information

The following information is given :

Name – Name of the museum in question.
Location – Nearest town/village and county.
Address – Postal address for museum.
Where – Directions to the museum in question by car.
Telephone – Telephone (and fax if applicable) number of the museum. This number is usually office hours. If available at other times, this will be stated.
Open – Opening times and days correct at the time of going to press.
By bus – Details of local bus services that go near to the museum. More details from the TIC – see below.
By rail – Nearest railway (or tube) station with as-the-crow-flies distance to the museum.
Tourist – Telephone (and fax if applicable) of the local Tourist Information Centre to which general enquires can be made. TIC's can provide a vast range of information, including details of places to visit within a 50 miles radius; accommodation; restaurants, cafes etc; travel information etc. In general, they are open Monday to Friday 9am to 5pm, with longer hours, including weekend opening, during the summer months. A TIC marked * is not open all year. In that case, the nearest all-year alternative is given, or make enquires of the appropriate Regional Tourist Board.

Admission – Admission prices correct at the time of going to press. Discounts for larger parties may also apply, please check with the museum in question.

Facilities – It would be an impossible task to list every facility available. Some of the more practical ones have been itemised. As before, make enquiries with the museum involved before setting out if you are unsure of anything.

Toilets	Toilets/washroom facilities on site.
Parking	Museum has its own car park.
Cafe	Catering facilities on site. These may range from a drinks/food vending machines to cafe facilities to restaurant, or combinations of such facilities. Use the museum 'phone number to check if unsure.
Shop	Gift shop or similar on site. Again, this may vary in size and in the range of items stocked.
Disabled	Facilities for the disabled. If in doubt, enquire of the museum on the telephone number given.
Kids	Children's play area or similar on site.
All	Considered to be a genuine 'all-weather' venue, ie the museum offers extensive areas undercover and that a visit in poor weather would not totally ruin the trip.
Changes	Supporting displays regularly changed so that a visit a year later would give the public something different to see.
Brochure	Sending a large stamped addressed envelope to the museum address given will bring an information leaflet by return.
X	Museum did not reply to the questionnaire sent to them.

* Any of the above codes shown with an asterisk (eg Disabled*) signifies a partial facility, eg disabled access not possible to all areas.

Note: *All facilities are listed in good faith and using the most up-to-date information available to the compiler. Visitors are urged to telephone ahead with specific enquires to avoid disappointment.*

Museum Narrative

A brief description of the museum is given in narrative form. This will include a general description of the collecting policy of the museum, special features and items of interest. Readers are reminded that displays, special features and aircraft exhibits may change at quite short notice. To avoid disappointment, contact the museum in question before setting out if you are seeking a specific item.

Aircraft Exhibit Tables

Column 1 – Aircraft are listed in alpha-numeric order, with civilian aircraft first, then military, then aircraft that carry no form of identification marking. A number in quotation marks indicates that it carries spurious markings.

Column 2 – Manufacturer, name, designation and marque number. With rarer types, some further explanation (eg homebuilt, man-powered aircraft, replica etc) is given, where space permits. Incomplete aircraft (cockpit sections, nose sections, fuselage etc) are also denoted here. Original design houses are used for the naming of each type. If space permits, licence manufacturers etc are given in brackets. It has been necessary to abbreviate some manufacturers names, as follows :

ANEC	Air Navigation & Engineering Co
BA	British Klemm Aeroplane Co
BAC	British Aircraft Corporation
BP	Boulton Paul
CASA	Construcciones Aeronauticas SA
DH	de Havilland
DHA	de Havilland Australia
DHC	de Havilland Canada
EE	English Electric
FMA	Fábrica Militar de Aviones
GD	General Dynamics
HP	Handley Page
HS	Hawker Siddeley
LVG	Luft Verkehrs Gesellschaft
MiG	Mikoyan-Gurevich
MS	Morane Saulnier
McDD	McDonnell Douglas
NA	North American
RAF	Royal Aircraft Factory
SAAB	Svenska Aeroplan AB
SAL	Scottish Aviation Ltd
SNIAS	Société Nationale Industrielle Aérospatiale
Sup	Supermarine

The evolution of names for manufacturers during the production life of an aircraft type can be a minefield for compilers of works such as this guide. Some latitude has been given which may upset purists. For example, the Buccaneer S.1 has been attributed to Blackburn, but the S.2 to Hawker Siddeley. The main aim has been to avoid such horrors as 'BAe Spitfire' which have crept into other reference works!

Beyond this appears information in brackets that may help the visitor to further identify an exhibit. Items in *rounded* brackets may give a real identity (if a spurious one is given in Column 1) or other form of identity not worn on the airframe. A common example of the latter is a British Aviation Preservation Council (BAPC) identity number, applied to aircraft that lack any other form of identity. Items in *squared* brackets relate to prominent code markings worn on aircraft, eg [8-NY] or [NN-D]. The symbol ✈ is used to denote an aircraft airworthy at time of going to press. **Column 3** Gives country of origin and year of manufacture. Country of origin is that of the *original* design house.

The following abbreviations apply :

Arg	Argentina
Aus	Austria
Aust	Australia
Bel	Belgium
Can	Canada
Fr	France
Gr	Germany
It	Italy
Ja	Japan
Pol	Poland
Ru	Russia, ie the former USSR
Sp	Spain
Swn	Sweden
Sws	Switzerland
US	United States of America

As the vast majority of aircraft exhibits in British museums are of British origin, if a country of origin code is not given, then it is British. Where a year of manufacture is prefixed with a 'c' (eg c75) this denotes an approximation. To save space, years have had the '19' removed, except for 19th century dates. With replicas, the year of manufacture is given for the original type upon which the replica was based – as this gives a better indication of the era the museum is striving to illustrate. Prefixing this information may be the symbol § which indicates that at the time of going to press the aircraft was stored (perhaps not even on site) or otherwise, and not available for public inspection. For major collections (eg the Fleet Air Arm Museum, RAF Museum) with extensive off-site storage facilities, no attempt has been made to list stored airframes.

Also...
Details of other events staged at the venue and items of interest etc staged in the immediate vicinity. (If applicable)

Nearby...
Details of other museums, interesting venues etc within a 20 mile radius of the museum in question. A particular leaning towards transport and industrial museums etc has been adopted. This section is designed to provide hints to help plan a full day (or weekend, or holiday) within the area – greater details from the TIC. Venues listed are not intended to be comprehensive and inevitably reflect the whims of the compiler. Distances given are as-the-crow-flies. Comments from readers as to other venues to be included in the next edition are very welcome.

Also in...
Where applicable, details are given of other aviation items of interest within the region. These will include collections that are not open to the general public on a regular basis and that require prior permission, but happily entertain visitors on this basis.

Important
The information contained in this guide is given in good faith on the basis of information submitted to, and research by, the compiler. Every effort has been made to be as accurate as possible. However, neither the compiler nor the Publishers can be held responsible for any errors, misinterpretations or omissions that may occur. All liability for loss, disappointment, negligence or other damage caused by reliance on the information contained in this guide is hereby excluded.

EAST ANGLIA

Bedfordshire, Cambridgeshire, Essex, Hertfordshire, Norfolk, Suffolk

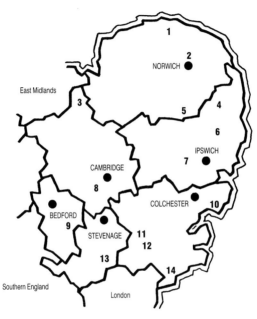

1 Muckleborough Collection
2 City of Norwich Aviation Museum
3 Fenland Aviation Museum
4 Norfolk & Suffolk Aviation Museum
5 100th BG Memorial Museum
6 390th BG Memorial Museum
7 Rebel Air Museum
8 Imperial War Museum, Duxford
9 Shuttleworth Collection
10 East Essex Aviation Museum
11 North Weald Airfield Museum
12 Blake Hall
13 Mosquito Aircraft Museum
14 Thameside Aviation Museum

East Anglia Tourist Board
Toppesfield Hall, Hadleigh, Suffolk, IP7 5DN
Tel: 01473 822922 Fax: 01473 823063

BLAKE HALL 'OPS' ROOM AND AIRSCENE MUSEUM

Chipping Ongar, Essex

Address: Blake Hall, Bovinger, nr Ongar, Essex.
Telephone: 01277 363328.
Where: Near Bovinger, north of the A414 Harlow to Chipping Ongar Road. Junction 7 off the M11.
Open: Daily 11am to 5pm, Easter to October.
By bus: Buses serve North Weald Bassett and Chipping Ongar.
By rail: Epping Underground, Central Line, 5 mls
Tourist: Chelmsford 01245 283400, Fax 01245 354026. Saffron Walden 01799 510444.
Admission: Adult £1.50, Child 50p.
Facilities: Toilets/Parking/Shop/Kids/All/ Changes/Brochure.

Within this fine 17th century house, which also has famous gardens open to the public, was located the operations room for the RAF's 'Sector E' after it was bombed at the nearby North Weald airfield. The 'ops' room with its status boards, plotter charts, viewing balcony etc have all been lovingly restored since 1984 to produce a unique museum. The Airscene Museum extends the story still further with a wealth of display material. Guided tours provide for a very personal visit.

Nearby:

Central London, *20 miles*.
North Weald Airfield Museum, *3 miles, page 17*.
Hatfield House, *18 miles*
Mosquito Aircraft Museum, *20 miles*.
Museum of Artillery, *18 miles, page 37*.
RAF Museum, *20 miles, page 38*.
Thameside Aviation Museum, *20 miles, page 22*.

EAST ESSEX AVIATION MUSEUM AND MUSEUM OF THE 1940s near St Osyth, Essex

Address: M Gadd, 32 Key Road, Clacton, Essex, CO15 3DA.
Where: Within the Point Clear Caravan Park at the end of an unclassified road from St Osyth, west of Clacton-on-Sea.
Open: Open Mondays 7pm to 10pm and Sundays 10am to 2pm. June to September open additionally Wednesdays and Thursdays 10am to 2pm. Hoping to extend open times, send SAE for details.
By bus: Bus service from Clacton to the Caravan Park.
By rail: Clacton, 5 miles.
Tourist: Clacton 01255 423400.
Admission: Free – donations welcomed.
Facilities: Toilets*/Parking/Cafe*/Shop/Kids*/ All/Changes/Brochure.

Located within a coastline look-out Martello tower, the museum includes a wealth of material on wartime aerial activity in the area, including many items recovered from the sea and local crash sites. Dominating this is the very complete wreckage of a Mustang that crashed off-shore in January 1945. As well as the many aviation artefacts, there are displays showing life in wartime Essex. There are toilets, a cafe and 'diversions' for children within the Caravan Park.

Aircraft exhibit:

☐	44-14574 NA P-51D Mustang wreck	US '44

Nearby:

Clacton-on-Sea, *5 miles*.
Clacton Aerodrome, *(pleasure flying, viewing area) 5 miles*.
Maritime Museum, *Harwich 16 miles*.
Rebel Air Museum, *20 miles – see page 19*.

FENLAND AVIATION MUSEUM

near Wisbech, Cambridgeshire

Address: Richard Mason, 63 St Leonard's Road, Leverington, Wisbech, Cambs, PE13 5BA.
Where: Located at Bamber's Garden Centre, Old Lynn Road, West Walton Highway, near Wisbech – off the A47/B198 junction and signposted from the A47.
Open: Weekends and Bank Holidays, March to September 9.30am to 5pm.
By bus: Peterborough to King's Lynn service passes the museum gates.
By rail: King's Lynn, 10 miles.
Tourist: Wisbech 01945 583 263, Fax 01945 582784.
Admission: Adult £1, child/cons 50p.
Facilities: Toilets/Parking/Cafe/Shop/Disabled/Kids/All/Changes/Brochure.

Run by the Fenland Aircraft Preservation Society, the museum is centred around a growing collection of aircraft – for which a hangar appeal is under way and an astounding collection of aircraft engines and exhibits illustrating the history of military aviation in the Fens. The museum is well known for its restoration to pristine condition of aero engines salvaged from crash sites and has won a major award for the restoration of a Vampire. The garden centre's facilities are available to museum visitors, including a tea room and an aquatic centre.

Aircraft exhibits:

☐ G-ARNH	Piper Colt 108	§ US '61
☐ XD434	DH Vampire T.11	'54
☐ XE998	DH Vampire T.11	§ '55
☐ XP488	Slingsby Grasshopper TX.1	§ '62
☐ XS420	EE Lightning T.5	'65
☐ XS459	EE Lightning T.5	'65

Nearby:

King's Lynn, *12 miles.*
Long Sutton Butterfly and Falconry Park, *8 miles.*
Sandringham, *16 miles.*
Wildfowl Trust, *Peakirk 20 miles.*
Wisbech Museum, *2 miles.*

XS420, one of Fenland's pair of Lightning T.5s during its time with 226 OCU at Coltishall, Norfolk, *circa* 1967.
MAP

IMPERIAL WAR MUSEUM

Duxford, Cambridgeshire

Address: Duxford Airfield, Duxford, Cambs, CB2 4QR.

Telephone: 01223 835000, Events Hotline 0891 516816, Fax 01223 837267.

Open: Daily 10am to 6pm April to October and 10am to 4pm the remainder of the year. Last admission 45 minutes before closing. Closed New Year's Day and December 24-26.

By bus: On various bus routes, details from TIC.

By rail: Whittlesford 3 miles.

Tourist: Cambridge 01223 322640, Fax 01223 463385.

Admission: Adult £6, OAP £4, child/cons £3, Family ticket £17. Charges differ for special event days.

Facilities: Toilets/Parking/Cafe/Shop/Disabled/ Kids/All/Changes/Brochure.

Run in conjunction with the Duxford Aviation Society (DAS) and Cambridgeshire County Council, Duxford is a huge and vibrant centre which benefits from being on a 'live' airfield. The Imperial War Museum (IWM – see also South Lambeth, London) has the majority of its aircraft collection at Duxford, and offers views of aircraft under restoration. Not just aircraft, the impressive Land Warfare Exhibition Hall (with connecting light railway) contains a large array of vehicles in battlefield scenes. Frequent special exhibitions are staged and Duxford is often used for rallies, fly-ins etc. Duxford was a former fighter base and the Operations Room has been restored to its Battle of Britain guise. Simulator rides* and pleasure flying* also available. There are several airshows* during the year, crowned by the Flying Legends display each July. Most days two of the DAS collection of civil airliners, normally including Concorde, are available for public inspection. Duxford is home to a wide range of classic aircraft and 'warbird' operators and their aircraft can frequently be seen flying or under maintenance, during a visit or airshow. Resident operators include: the Aircraft Restoration Company, B-17 Preservation Ltd, Classic Wings, The Fighter Collection, Old Flying Machine Company and Plane Sailing Ltd.   * Extra charges apply.

Aircraft exhibits:

CF-KCG	Grumman TBM-3E Avenger	US '44
☐ D-CACY	Hawker Sea Fury FB.11	'50
☐ G-AFBS	Miles Magister I	'39
☐ G-AGJG	DH Dragon Rapide	§ '41
☐ G-AGTO	Auster J/1 Autocrat →	'45
☐ G-AIYR	DH Dragon Rapide →	'44

G-ALZO, the only surviving Airspeed Ambassador, at Gatwick in the 1960s. Peter J Bish

☐ G-AKAZ	Piper L-4A Grasshopper ✈ [HL-6¼]	US	'42
☐ G-ALDG	HP Hermes 4 fuselage		'49
☐ G-ALFU	DH Dove 6		'48
☐ G-ALWF	Vickers Viscount 701		'52
☐ G-ALZO	Airspeed Ambassador		'50
☐ G-ANTK	Avro York		'46
☐ G-AOVT	Bristol Britannia 312		'58
☐ G-APDB	DH Comet 4		'58
☐ G-APWJ	HP Herald 201		'59
☐ G-ASGC	Vickers Super VC-10		'63
☐ G-ASTG	Nord 1002 Pingouin	§ Fr	'45
☐ G-AVFB	HS Trident 2E		'68
☐ G-AVMU	BAC 111-510ED		'69
☐ G-AWAH	Beech Baron D55 ✈		'68
☐ G-AXDN	BAC/SNIAS Concorde 101	UK/Fr	'71
☐ G-AZMH	MS.500 Criquet ✈	Fr	'51
☐ G-AZSC	NA Harvard IIB ✈	US	'43
☐ G-BOML	Hispano HA-1112 Buchon ✈	Sp	c'52
☐ G-USUK	Colt 2500A balloon gondola		'87
☐ D-HDME	Messerschmitt Bf 109G-10 ([2]	Gr	c42
☐ LN-AMY	NA AT-6D Harvard ✈	US	'44
☐ N47DD	Republic P-47D Thunderbolt	§ US	'44
☐ NX700HL	Grumman F8F Bearcat ✈	US	'45
☐ NX5224R	Yakovlev Yak-50 ✈	Ru	c77
☐ N4845V	Grumman FM-2 Wildcat ✈ [F]	US	'42
☐ N7614C	NA B-25J Mitchell	US	'44
☐ N9938	Hispano HA-1112 Buchon	§ Sp	c52
☐ VR-BPS	Consolidated PBY-5A Catalina ✈	US	'44
☐ 'A1742'	Bristol Scout replica (BAPC.38)	§	'15
☐ 'D8084'	Bristol F.2b Fighter (G-ACAA)		'18
☐ E2581	Bristol F.2b Fighter		'18
☐ F3556	RAF RE.8		'18
☐ N5903	Gloster Gladiator II (G-GLAD)		'40
☐ N4877	Avro Anson I (G-AMDA) [VX-F]		'38
☐ V3388	Airspeed Oxford I (G-AHTW)		'40
☐ 'V6028'	Bristol Bolingbroke IVT (G-MKIV)	§	'42
☐ 'V9673'	Westland Lysander III (G-LIZY) [MA-J]		c43
☐ 'W2068'	Avro Anson I [68]		§ c38
☐ Z2033	Fairey Firefly I (G-ASTL) [275]		'44
☐ 'Z5722'	Bristol Bolingbroke IVT ✈ (G-BPIV) [WM-Z]		'42
☐ Z7015	Hawker Sea Hurricane I (G-BKTH)		'41
☐ 'Z7381'	Hawker Hurricane XII ✈ (G-HURI) [XR-T]		c43
☐ FE992	NA Harvard IIB ✈ (G-BDAM)		'42
☐ HM580	Cierva C.30A (G-ACUU)	Sp	'34
☐ KB889	Avro Lancaster X (G-LANC) [NA-I]		'44
☐ KF487	NA Harvard IIB	§ US	'45
☐ KL161	NA Mitchell II ✈ (N88972) [VO-B]	US	
☐ KZ321	Hawker Hurricane IV (G-HURY)	§	'43
☐ LZ766	Percival Proctor III (G-ALCK)		'44
☐ MH434	Sup Spitfire IX ✈ (G-ASJV) [ZD-B]		'43
☐ ML407	Sup Spitfire Tr IX ✈ (G-LFIX) [OU-V]		'44
☐ ML417	Sup Spitfire IX ✈ (G-BJSG) [21-T]		'44
☐ ML796	Short Sunderland MR.5		'44
☐ MV293	Sup Spitfire XIV ✈ (G-SPIT) [OI-C]		'45
☐ NF370	Fairey Swordfish II		'44
☐ PK624	Supermarine Spitfire F.22 [RAU-T]		'45
☐ PL965	Sup Spitfire PR.XI ✈ (G-MKXI)		'44
☐ RK858	Supermarine Spitfire IX	§	'44
☐ RN201	Supermarine Spitfire XIV (G-BSKP)	§	'45
☐ TA719	DH Mosquito TT.35 (G-ASKC) [6T]		'45
☐ TG528	HP Hastings C.1A		'47
☐ TV959	DH Mosquito T.3	§	'45
☐ TX226	Avro Anson C.19	§	'46
☐ VN485	Supermarine Spitfire F.24		'45
☐ VT260	Gloster Meteor F.4	§	'48
☐ VX653	Hawker Sea Fury FB.11 (G-BUCM)		'49
☐ 'WF714'	Gloster Meteor F.8 (WK914)	§	'53
☐ WH725	EE Canberra B.2		'53
☐ WJ945	Vickers Varsity T.1 (G-BEDV)		'53
☐ WK991	Gloster Meteor F.8		'53
☐ WM969	Hawker Sea Hawk FB.5		'54
☐ WZ590	DH Vampire T.11 [19]		'52
☐ XB261	Blackburn Beverley C.1 cockpit		'55
☐ XE627	Hawker Hunter F.6A [T]		'56
☐ XF375	Hawker Hunter F.6 (G-BUEZ) [05]	§	'57
☐ XF708	Avro Shackleton MR.3/3 [C]		'58
☐ XG613	DH Sea Venom FAW.21		'56
☐ XG797	Fairey Gannet ECM.6 [766-BY]		'57
☐ XH648	HP Victor B.1A (K2P)		'59
☐ XH897	Gloster Javelin FAW.9		'58
☐ XJ676	Hawker Hunter F.6A	§	'57
☐ XJ824	Avro Vulcan B.2		'61
☐ XK936	Westland Whirlwind HAS.7 [62]	US	'57
☐ XM135	EE Lightning F.1		'59
☐ XN239	Slingsby Cadet TX.3		c57
☐ XP281	Auster AOP.9		'61

☐	XP772	DHC Beaver AL.1 (G-BUCJ)	§ Can '61	☐	'152/17'	Fokker Dr I replica ✈ (G-ATJM)	Gr '17
☐	XR222	BAC TSR-2	'64	☐	243	Hawker Fury ISS ✈ (G-BTTA)	'49
☐	XR241	Auster AOP.9 ✈ (G-AXRR)	'61	☐	'1164'	Beech 18 3TM ✈ (G-BKGL)	US '46
☐	XS183	Hunting Jet Provost T.4	§ '63	☐	3794	MiG MiG-15 (S-102)	§ c52
☐	XS567	Westland Wasp HAS.1 [434-E]	'64	☐	6247	MiG MiG-15UTI (SBLim-2A) ✈	
☐	XS576	DH Sea Vixen FAW.2 [125 -E]	'64			(G-OMIG)	Ru c55
☐	XS863	Westland Wessex HAS.1	US '65	☐	8178	NA F-86A Sabre (G-SABR)	US '48
☐	XV474	McDD Phantom FGR.2 [T]	US '70	☐	9893	Bristol Bolingbroke IVT	§ '42
☐	XW763	HS Harrier GR.3 fuselage	§ '72	☐	10639	Messerschmitt Bf 109G-2 ✈	
☐	XZ133	HS Harrier GR.3	'75			(G-USTV) [6]	Gr '43
☐	A-549	FMA Pucara	Arg c76	☐	14286	Lockheed T-33A 'T-Bird'	US '51
☐	A8-324	Bristol Beaufighter 21	'44	☐	18393	Avro Canada CF.100 Mk IV	
☐	A68-192	NA Mustang 22 ((G-HAEC)	US '45			(G-BCYK)	Can '55
☐	B-168	NA Harvard IIB	§ US '42	☐	'20385'	NA Harvard IV (G-BGPB)	§ c44
☐	E3B-153	CASA 1-131E Jungmann ✈		☐	'40467'	Grumman F6F-5K Hellcat ✈	
☐		(G-BPTS)	Sp c52			(G-BTCC)	US '43
	Fv16105	NA Harvard IIB (G-BTXI)	US '42	☐	'42161'	Lockheed T-33A-3 Silver Star ✈	
☐	Fv35075	SAAB J35A Draken	Swn c60			(N33VC)	US c54
☐	'MM53211'	Fiat G.46-IV (BAPC.79)	§ It c49	☐	42165	NA F-100D Super Sabre	US '54
☐	NZ5648	Vought FG-1D Corsair ✈ (NX55JP)	US '44	☐	60689	Boeing B-52D Stratofortress	US '56
☐	'S4523'	SPAD S.XIII (N4727V)	Fr '18	☐	66692	Lockheed U-2CT	US '56
☐	'20'	Lavochkin La-11	§ Ru c45	☐	67543	Lockheed P-38J Lightning ✈	
☐	'36'	Yakovlev C-11 ✈ (G-KYAK)	Ru '50			(NX3145X)	US '42
☐	'53'	Curtiss P-40B Warhawk	US '41	☐	88297	Vought FG-1D Corsair ✈ (G-FGID)	US '44
☐	57	Dassault Mystère IVA [8-MT]	Fr '55	☐	100143	Focke-Achgelis Fa 330A-1	Gr c43
☐	'69'	Yakovlev Yak-50 ✈ (G-BTZB)	Ru c77			rotorkite	

☐	'124485'	Boeing B-17G Flying Fortress ✈	
		(G-BEDF)	US '45
☐	126922	Douglas AD-4NA Skyraider ✈	
		(G-RAID)	US c50
☐	155574	McDD F-4J(UK) Phantom [J]	US '67
☐	0-17899	Convair VT-29B-CO Samaritan	§ US '51
☐	191660	Messerschmitt Me 163B-1 Komet [3]	Gr '44
☐	'226671'	Republic P-47D\N Thunderbolt ✈	
		(NX47DD)	US '44
☐	'231983'	Boeing B-17G Flying Fortress	
		(F-BDRS) [IY-G]	US '45
☐	269097	Bell P-63A Kingcobra ✈ (G-BTWR)	US '43
☐	315509	Douglas C-47A Skytrain (G-BHUB)	US '43
☐	461748	Boeing TB-29A Superfortress	
		(G-BHDK)	US '44
☐	'463221'	NA P-51D Mustang ✈ (G-BTCD)	US '44
☐	67-0120	GD F-111E	US '67
☐	77-0259	Fairchild A-10A Thunderbolt II	US '77

Left: Cierva C.30A autogiro restored to its wartime markings, serving in the radar calibration role with 529 Squadron. *Imperial War Museum.*
Below: **Classic Wings offer sight-seeing flights around the Duxford circuit and further afield, using their DH Dragon Rapide G-AIYR.** *Classic Wings*

☐	–	Amiot AAC.1 Toucan (Ju 52) (6316)	
		[IZ+NK]	Gr c49
☐	–	Boeing PT-17 Kaydet	§ US c42
☐	–	Bristol Beaufighter I nose	c40
☐	–	Bücker Bü 133C Jungmeister ✈	
		(G-AYSJ) [LG+01]	Gr c38
☐	–	DH Tiger Moth frame	§ c41
☐	–	DHC Chipmunk T.10 fuselage	Can c52
☐	–	DHC Chipmunk T.10 fuselage	Can c52
☐	–	Fieseler Fi 103 (V-1) on launch ramp	
		(BAPC.93)	Gr c44
☐	–	Hawker Typhoon cockpit	c42
☐	–	MS.502 Criquet (EI-AUY)	Fr c51
☐	–	MS.505 Criquet ✈ (G-BPHZ)	
		[TA+RC]	Fr c55
☐	–	NA P-51 Mustang rep [88]	§ US c44
☐	–	Nakajima Ki-43 Hayabusa	Ja c43

Nearby:

Audley End House (and miniature railway), *6 miles.*
Cambridge Museum of Technology, *8 miles.*
City of Cambridge, *8 miles.*
Shuttleworth Collection, *20 miles – see page 19.*
Stretham Old Engine House, *18 miles.*
Wimpole Home Farm, *6 miles.*

The prototype de Havilland Mosquito, built at London Colney and first flown on 25th November 1940. Roger Richards

MOSQUITO AIRCRAFT MUSEUM

London Colney, Herts

Address: PO Box 107, Salisbury Hall, London Colney, near St Albans, Herts, AL2 1BU.
Telephone: 01727 822051.
Where: At Salisbury Hall, on the B556 west of the South Mimms services (junction of A1/M25). Access off M25 junction 22 (signposted).
Open: March to the end of October, Tuesdays, Thursdays and Saturdays 2pm to 5.30pm, Sundays and Bank Holidays 10.30am to 5.30pm. Last admission 4.30pm.
By bus: No 84 from St Albans to New Barnet stops at end of drive.
By rail: St Albans 4 miles.
Tourist: St Albans 01727 864511, Fax 01727 863533.
Admission: Adult £3, child/OAP £1.
Facilities: Toilets/Parking/Shop/Disabled/All/ Brochure.

Set in the grounds of Salisbury Hall (not available for inspection) the museum is devoted to the history of the de Havilland company and associated operations, including Airspeed. The Hall was used as a satellite design and development facility for nearby Hatfield airfield during the war and indeed the prototype Mosquito was built here. As well as the large aircraft display hall, there is a workshop and an engine display room plus static aircraft park. Several aircraft in 'working' order (undercarriage retraction, wing folding etc) and there are days when these are put through their paces. Some aircraft are held on the former Hatfield airfield and can only be viewed 'from afar' for the time being.

Aircraft exhibits:

☐ D-IFSB	DH Dove 6	'53
☐ F-BCDB	DH Dragon Rapide	'45
☐ G-ABLM	Cierva C.24 autogyro	'31
☐ G-ADOT	DH Hornet Moth	'35
☐ G-AFOJ	DH Moth Minor	'39
☐ G-ANRX	DH Tiger Moth crop duster	'39
☐ G-AOJT	DH Comet 1XB fuselage	'53

☐ G-AOTI	DH Heron 2D	§ '53
☐ G-AREA	DH Dove 8	§ '60
☐ G-ARYC	HS.125 Srs 1	'62
☐ G-AVFH	HS Trident 2 nose	'68
☐ G-AWZO	HS Trident 3B-101	§ '72
☐ W4050	DH Mosquito I prototype	'40
☐ LF789	DH Queen Bee (BAPC.186)	c43
☐ TA122	DH Mosquito FB.6 [UP-G]	'45
☐ TA634	DH Mosquito TT.35 [8K-K]	'45
☐ TJ118	DH Mosquito TT.35 nose	'45
☐ WM729	DH Vampire NF.10 nose	'52
☐ WP790	DHC Chipmunk T.10 (G-BBNC) [T]	Can '52
☐ WR539	DH Venom FB.4 [F]	§ '56
☐ WX853	DH Venom NF.3	'55
☐ XD616	DH Vampire T.11	'55
☐ XE985	DH Vampire T.11	§ '54

☐ XG730	DH Sea Venom FAW.22 [499-A]	'57
☐ XJ565	DH Sea Vixen FAW.2 [127-E]	'60
☐ XJ772	DH Vampire T.11	'55
☐ J-1008	DH Vampire FB.6	c55
☐ –	Hatfield Toucan man-powered aircraft , frame (BAPC.146)	'72
☐ –	Airspeed Horsa I / II fuselage (BAPC.232)	'43

Nearby:
Blake Hall, *20 miles – see page 8.*
Central London, *16 miles.*
Hatfield House, *6 miles.*
North Weald Airfield and Museum, *20 miles.*
RAF Museum, Hendon, *10 miles – see page 38.*
Verulamium Roman Town, *6 miles.*

MUCKLEBURGH COLLECTION
Weybourne, Norfolk

Address: Weybourne Camp, Weybourne, Norfolk, NR25 7EG.
Telephone: 01263 588210, Fax 01263 588425.
Where: Signposted off the A149 west of Cromer.
Open: Mid-March to October 10am to 5pm daily and weekends only winter 10am to 5pm.
By bus: Coastal bus service from Sheringham.
By rail: Sheringham 3 miles.
Tourist: Sheringham* 01263 824329. Cromer 01263 512497.
Admission: Adult £3, OAP £2.70, child £1.80, family ticket £7.90.
Facilities: Toilets/Parking/Cafe/Shop/Disabled/ Kids/All/Changes/Brochure.

Located on the site of the former Weybourne Military Camp is Britain's largest private military collection including over 100 military vehicles and armoured fighting vehicles from the UK and abroad including the former USSR, Kuwait, Syria, and the Falklands. Other exhibitions include the tank hall, a yeomanry exhibition, naval and maritime display including a major feature devoted to the RNLI. There are working demonstration days when a variety of tanks and vehicles are driven on Bank Holidays, Sundays and daily throughout August. A 'Gama Goat' US Marine Corps amphibious carrier undertakes coastal tours (extra charge) during the main season. As well as the airframes, the museum has Bloodhound, Thunderbird and and Skybolt missiles on show.

Aircraft exhibits:

☐ WD686	Gloster Meteor NF.11	'52
☐ XZ968	HS Harrier GR.3	'82

Nearby:
City of Norwich Aviation Museum, *20 miles – see page 18.*
Cromer, *6 miles.*
North Norfolk Railway, *2 miles.*
Thursford Steam Museum, *8 miles.*
Wells and Walsingham Light Railway, *10 miles.*
See over.

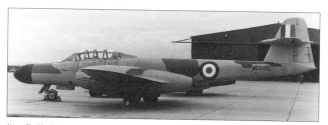

Above: **The Muckleburgh Collection's Meteor NF.11 operational at Llanbedr, 1960.** MAP.

NORFOLK AND SUFFOLK AVIATION MUSEUM

Flixton, Suffolk

Address: Huby Fairhead, 48 Monks Cottages, Langley, Norwich, Norfolk, NR14 8DG.
Telephone: 01986 896644 during museum opening hours.
Where: On the B1062 south west of Bungay.
Open: Easter to October, Sundays and Bank Holidays 10am to 5pm; July to August Tuesday, Wednesdays and Thursdays 10am to 5pm.
By bus: Services to Bungay 2 miles.
By train: Beccles 8 miles.
Tourist: Beccles* 01502 713196. Diss 01379 650523, Fax 01379 31141.

Admission: Free, donations welcomed.
Facilities: Toilets/Parking/Shop/Disabled*/All/ Changes/Brochure.

Well established and growing collection of aircraft and artefacts illustrating the development of aviation in general and in particular World War Two flying from Norfolk and Suffolk. Within the museum is the Royal Observer Corps Museum dedicated to telling the story of the Corps from its earliest days up to its 'stand down'. Good display of artefacts including much from surrounding USAAF bases. Large display and restoration hangar.

Aircraft exhibits:

☐ G-AZLM	Cessna F.172L fuselage		US '71
☐ G-MTFK	Flexiform Striker microlight		'87
☐ N99153	NA T-28C Trojan fuselage		US '53
☐ 'P8140'	Sup Spitfire replica (BAPC.71) [ZP-K]		'40
☐ VL349	Avro Anson C.19		'46

Below: **Development Lightning F.1 XG329 outside Flixton's aircraft display hangar.** Ken Ellis

☐ VX580	Vickers Valetta C.2	'50
☐ WF128	Percival Sea Prince T.1	'52
☐ WF643	Gloster Meteor F.8	'51
☐ WH840	EE Canberra T.4	'54
☐ WV605	Percival Provost T.1 [T-B]	'54
☐ XG329	EE Lightning F.1	'59
☐ XH892	Gloster Javelin FAW.9R	'60
☐ XJ482	DH Sea Vixen FAW.1 [713-VL]	'58
☐ XK624	DH Vampire T.11 [32]	'56
☐ XM279	EE Canberra B(I).8 nose	'59
☐ XN304	Westland Whirlwind HAS.7 [F]	US '60
☐ XR485	Westland Whirlwind HAR.10 [Q]	US '64
☐ A-528	FMA Pucara	Arg c76
☐ 79	Dassault Mystère IVA [8-NB]	Fr '55
☐ 42196	NA F-100D Super Sabre	US '54
☐ 54433	Lockheed T-33A 'T-Bird'	US '55

☐ –		Bensen B.7 gyroglider (BAPC.147)	
		[LHS-1]	US c55
☐ –		Fokker D.VIII scale rep (BAPC.239)	Gr '18

Nearby:
Caister Castle Car Collection, *20 miles.*
City of Norwich Aviation Museum, *18 miles –*
  see page 18.
East Anglia Transport Museum, Carlton Colville,
  12 miles.
Great Yarmouth, *18 miles.*
Motor Museum and Zoo, Banham, *17 miles.*
Steam Museum, Buckenham, *12 miles.*
100th BG Museum, Thorpe Abbotts, *10 miles –*
  see page 23.
391st BG Museum, Framlingham, *18 miles –*
  see page 23.

NORTH WEALD
AIRFIELD MUSEUM
North Weald, Essex

Address: Ad Astra House, Hurricane Way, North
  Weald Aerodrome, Epping, Essex, CM16 6AA.
Telephone: 01992 572705, Fax 01992 523161.
Where: North Weald Bassett, on the B181 south
  east of Harlow, junction 7 M11. *Ad Astra* House
  is off Hurricane Way, entrace to which is from
  North Weald *village* and *not* via the aerodrome
  entrance.
Open: Saturdays and Sundays midday noon to
  4pm. Other times by arrangement.
By bus: Buses from Epping and Chipping Ongar.
By rail: Epping Underground, Central Line.
Tourist: Chelmsford 01245 283400, Fax 0124
  354026. Saffron Walden 01799 510444.
Admission: £1 or £5 annual membership.
Facilities: Toilets/Parking/Shop/All/Changes/
  Brochure.

An extensive collection telling the rich history of
North Weald airfield. The museum is located in a
building near the main gate of what was the Battle
of Britain station. Large array of artefacts in three
rooms spanning 1916 to its closure in 1964.

Also:
On North Weald airfield is the **Aces High Flying
Museum** with a large array of aircraft, many of
which have 'starred' in films, eg Douglas Dakota III
G-DAKS, MiG-21PF 'Fishbed' 503 and NA TB-25J
Mitchell N9089Z. Viewable by prior permission,
contact: Aces High, 'The Ford', Ford Road, Chob-
ham, Surrey, GU24 8SS. Also **39 Restoration
Group** working on a series of aircraft (eg Gloster
Meteor TT.20 WM224) and artefacts. Viewable by
prior permission, contact: Neil Griggs, 16 Dukes
Close, North Weald, Epping, Essex, CM16 6DA.

Nearby:
Central London, *20 miles.*
Blake Hall, *3 miles – see page 8.*
Hatfield House, *18 miles*
Mosquito Aircraft Museum, *20 miles – see page
  14.*
Museum of Artillery, *18 miles – see page 37.*
RAF Museum, *20 miles – see page 38.*
Thameside Aviation Museum, *20 miles –*
  see page 22.

CITY OF NORWICH AVIATION MUSEUM

Norwich Airport, Norfolk

Address: Old Norwich Road, Horsham St Faith, Norwich, Norfolk, NR10 3JE.

Telephone: 01603 625309 – recorded message out-of-hours.

Where: Close to Norwich Airport, access from the A140 Cromer Road.

Open: Sundays and Bank Holidays April to October 10am to 5pm and Sundays November to March 10am to 3.30pm. During May, June, July and August additionally open evenings 7.30pm to dusk and Wednesdays 2pm to 5pm.

By rail: Norwich 3 miles.

Tourist: Norwich 01603 666071, Fax 01603 765389.

Admission: Adult £1.50, child/OAP 75p.

Facilities: Toilets/Parking/Cafe/Shop/All/ Changes/Brochure.

On the edge of Norwich Airport – affording views of the comings and goings – the City of Norwich Aviation Museum has a varied aircraft park. Dominating this is the Vulcan and visitors can climb up into the cockpit when staffing levels permit. The internal displays have come on considerably in recent years and are in a constant state of change. Emphasis of the internal displays are the history of Norwich Airport when it was RAF Horsham St Faith, military aviation in the area, on wartime life in and around Norwich and on aerial VCs.

Aircraft exhibits:

☐ G-ASKK	HP Herald 211		'63
☐ XD375	DH Vampire T.11		'53
☐ XH767	Gloster Javelin FAW.9 [A]		'59
☐ XM612	Avro Vulcan B.2		'64
☐ XP355	Westland Whirlwind HAR.10 (G-BEBC) [A]		US '62
☐ XP458	Slingsby Grasshopper TX.1	§	'63
☐ XP919	DH Sea Vixen FAW.2 [706-VL]	§	'63
☐ –	Supermarine Scimitar F.1 nose		c59
☐ 121	Dassault Mystère IVA [8-MY]	Fr	'55
16718	Lockheed T-33A 'T-Bird'	US	'51

Nearby:

City of Norwich, *3 miles.*
Great Yarmouth (pleasure flying), *20 miles*
Motor Museum and Zoo, Banham, *20 miles.*
Muckleburgh Collection, *20 miles – see page 15.*
Norfolk & Suffolk Aviation Museum, *18 miles – see page 16.*
Steam Museum, Buckenham, *9 miles.*
100th Bomb Group Museum, *20 miles – see page 23.*

Vulcan B.2 XM612 with 101 Squadron *circa* 1979. MAP

REBEL AIR MUSEUM / EARLS COLNE AVIATION MUSEUM
Earls Colne, Essex

Address: c/o Earls Colne Aerodrome, Earls Colne, Halstead, Essex.
Where: Earls Colne airfield, signposted off the B1024 north of Coggeshall.
Open: Saturdays, Sundays and Bank Holidays April to October 10am to 6pm and other times by appointment.
By rail: Braintree 8 miles.
Tourist: Braintree 01376 550066.
Facilities: Toilets/Parking/Cafe*/Shop/Disabled*/ All/Changes/X

On the active Earls Colne airfield and amid a blossoming sports and social complex, the museum occupies a large hangar-like building with a fascinating array of airframes, artefacts and displays. Heavy emphasis is placed upon the history of the airfields locally, including the B-26 Marauder operations of the USAAF's 9th Air Force. A series of detailed set-pieces show domestic life in the Blitz, down to period 'dolly tubs' and washing powders! Light aircraft park close by and the large sports centre offers a range of food and drink.

Aircraft exhibits:

☐ N9606H	Fairchild PT-26 Cornell II	US '42
☐ EE425	Gloster Meteor F.3 nose	'46
☐ –	Mignet HM.14 Flying Flea (BAPC.115)	Fr c36

Nearby:
Colchester, *10 miles.*
Colne Valley Railway, *8 miles.*
East Essex Aviation Museum, *20 miles – see page 8.*
Stour Valley Railway Centre, *4 miles.*

SHUTTLEWORTH COLLECTION
Old Warden, Bedfordshire

Address: Old Warden Aerodrome, Biggleswade, Beds, SG18 9ER.
Telephone: 01767 727288, Fax 01767 627745.
Where: East of the B658, west of Biggleswade. Well signposted, including from the A1.
Open: Daily throughout the year, but is closed for up to 14 days covering Xmas Eve, and up to and including New Year's Day. Open April to October 10am to 5pm, November to March 10am to 4pm, the hangar displays are closed one hour after the last admission time.
By rail: Biggleswade 3 miles.
Tourist: Bedford 01234 215226 (and fax).
Admission: Adult £5, child/OAP/cons £2.50. Different prices apply on flying days.
Facilities: Toilets/Parking/Cafe/Shop/Disabled/ Kids/All/Brochure.

Classic historic aircraft, the majority airworthy, nestled amid a delightful grass airfield – the Shuttleworth Collection has long had a heady atmosphere. There are five hangars containing the 'fleet' along with many supporting displays, including the age of airships, flying clothing and engines. A workshop allows visitors to monitor the restoration of collection aircraft. The garage and coachroom houses the impressive collection of vintage cars. On 'normal' days visitors might well be able to see light aircraft visiting the airfield, but the collection stages a series of flying days and evenings* during the summer season when many of the unique resident types take to the air and are joined by modern day military machines, 'warbirds' and other performers. The collection is also host to various fly-ins, classic and veteran car rallies, radio control model flying days and much more.
* Additional charges apply.

One of the airborne delights at Shuttleworth, the Hawker Tomtit trainer. Ken Ellis

Aircraft exhibits:

☐ G-EAGA	Sopwith Dove ✈	'20
☐ G-EBHX	DH Humming Bird ✈	'23
☐ G-EBIR	DH.51 ✈	'25
☐ G-EBJO	ANEC II ultralight	§ '24
☐ G-EBLV	DH Moth ✈	'25
☐ G-EBWD	DH.60X Moth ✈	'28
☐ G-AAIN	Parnall Elf II ✈	'29
☐ G-AAPZ	Desoutter	§ '31
☐ G-AAYX	Southern Martlet	§ '31
☐ G-ABAG	DH Moth ✈	'30
☐ G-ABVE	Arrow Active II ✈	'32
☐ G-ABXL	Granger Archaeopteryx–taxiable	'30
☐ G-ACSS	DH.88 Comet [34] taxiable	'33
☐ G-ADGP	Miles Hawk Speed Six ✈	'35
☐ G-AEBB	Mignet HM.14 Flying Flea taxiable	Fr '36
☐ G-AEOA	DH Puss Moth ✈	'36
☐ G-AFCL	BA Swallow II ✈	'37
☐ F904	RAF SE.5A ✈ (G-EBIA)	'18
☐ D8096	Bristol F.2b Fighter ✈ (G-AEPH)	'18
☐ H5199	Avro 504K ✈ (G-ADEV)	'20
☐ K1786	Hawker Tomtit ✈ (G-AFTA)	'29
☐ K3215	Avro Tutor ✈ (G-AHSA)	'31
☐ K4235	Cierva (Avro 671) C.30A (G-AHMJ) taxiable	Sp '37
☐ 'K5414'	Hawker Hind (Afghan) ✈ (G-AENP)	c37
☐ L8032	Gloster Gladiator I ✈ (G-AMRK) [HP-B]	'37
☐ 'N6181'	Sopwith Pup ✈ (G-EBKY)	'18
☐ 'N6290'	Sopwith Triplane ✈ (G-BOCK)	'17
☐ P6382	Miles Magister I ✈ (G-AJDR)	'40
☐ T6818	DH Tiger Moth II ✈ (G-ANKT)	'40
☐ W9385	DH Hornet Moth ✈ (G-ADND) [YG-L]	'36
☐ AR501	Sup Spitfire V ✈ (G-AWII) [NN-A]	'42
☐ 7198/18	LVG C.VI ✈ (G-AANJ)	Gr '18
☐ –	Blackburn Monoplane ✈ (G-AANI)	'12
☐ –	Blake Bluetit (BAPC.37)	§ c33
☐ –	Bleriot XI ✈ (G-AANG)	Fr '10
☐ –	Bristol Boxkite replica ✈ (G-ASPP)	'10
☐ –	Deperdussin Monoplane ✈ (G-AANH)	Fr '10
☐ –	English Electric Wren ✈ (G-EBNV)	'23
☐ –	Roe Triplane IV replica ✈ (G-ARSG)	'10

Also:

Next door to the collection is the famed Swiss Garden, one of the top ten gardens in the country with landscape design from the early 19th century in ten splendid acres.

Nearby:

City of Bedford, *8 miles.*

Watch Tower Museum, Bassingbourn –
    see page 24.

Woburn Abbey and Safari Park, *14 miles.*

Imperial War Museum, Duxford, *20 miles* –
    see page 10.

Luton Airport, (with spectator facilities), *16 miles.*

Santa Pod Raceway, *16 miles.*

Top: **Brothers in arms, LVG and Bristol F.2b, World
War One two seaters.**

Above: **Those Magnificent Men... Blackburn
Monoplane and Roe Triplane.**

Both Ken Ellis

THAMESIDE AVIATION MUSEUM
East Tilbury, Essex

Address: 80 Elm Road, Grays, Essex, RM17 6LD.
Where: At Coalhouse Fort, on an unclassified road, east of Tilbury
Open: Open on the last Sunday of the month from 12.30pm and at other times by arrangement.
By rail: Tilbury 3 miles.
Tourist: Thurrock 01708 863733, Fax 01708 862440.
Facilities: Parking/X

A small collection established in a coastal defensive point overlooking the Thames estuary. Apart from the airframes, the collection centres upon a large amount of material from 'digs' on wreck sites in and around Essex.

Aircraft exhibits:

☐ G-ADXS	Mignet HM.14 Flying Flea		Fr '35
☐ G-AVZO	Beagle Pup 100 fuselage		'67
☐ B-163	NA Harvard IIB		US '42
☐ 0446	MiG MiG-21UM nose		Ru c72

Nearby:
Blake Hall, *20 miles – see page 8.*
Chatham Dockyard, *10 miles.*
Medway Aircraft Preservation Society workshop, *10 miles – see page 80.*
North Weald Airfield Museum, *20 miles – see page 17.*
Shoreham Aircraft Preservation Society, *16 miles – see page 78.*
Southend-on-Sea, *14 miles.*

'The Fleeing Fly', Mignet HM.14 G-ADXS, was built in Southend and made its first flight on 15th December 1935.
Bill Hale

100TH BOMB GROUP MEMORIAL MUSEUM

Thorpe Abbotts, Norfolk

Address: 100th BG Association, Common Road, Dickleburgh, Diss, Norfolk, IP21 4PH.
Telephone: 01379 740708.
Where: Signed off the A143, east of Diss.
Open: Open 10am to 5pm weekends. Wednesdays 10am to 5pm during May to September. Closes 4,30pm October to April.
By rail: Diss 5 miles.
Tourist: Diss 01379 650523, Fax 01508 31141.
Admission: Free, donations appreciated.
Facilities: Toilets/Parking/Shop/Disabled*/All/ Changes/Brochure.

The museum is centred around the restored control tower on what was home to the USAAF's famous 'Bloody Hundredth' Bomb Group. A superb and well presented series of displays take the visitor through life on an American bomber base, while telling the specific tale of Thorpe Abbotts. The runways may have gone, but the feeling of nostalgia when looking out from the top of the control tower is enormous. Other original World War Two buildings contain further displays including restored engines and items from local crash sites. Special events and reunions frequently staged.

Nearby:
Banham Motor Museum and Zoo, *10 miles*.
Bressingham Steam Museum & Railways, *8 miles*.
City of Norwich, *18 miles*.
City of Norwich Aviation Museum, *20 miles – see page 18*.
Mechanical Music Museum, Cotton 12, *18 miles*.
Museum of East Anglia Life, Stowmarket, *20 miles*.
Norfolk & Suffolk Aviation Museum, *10 miles – see page 16*.
Thetford Wildlife Park, *20 miles*.
390th Bomb Group Museum, *14 miles – see opposite*.

390TH BOMB GROUP MEMORIAL AIR MUSEUM

Parham, Suffolk

Address: Colin Durrant, Museum Manager, 101 Avondale Road, Ipswich, Suffolk, IP3 9LA.
Telephone: 01473 711275.
Where: North of the A12 to the east of Saxmundham, signposted.
Open: 11am to 6pm on Sundays and Bank Holidays March through to October. Other times by prior appointment.
By bus: Eastern Counties service Ipswich-Aldeburgh runs close to the museum.
By rail: Saxmundham 4 miles.
Tourist: Aldeburgh* 01728 453637. Ipswich 01473 258070, Fax 01473 250951.
Admission: Free, donations welcomed.
Facilities: Toilets/Parking/Cafe/Shop/All/ Brochure.

Based upon the restored control tower of USAAF Station 153, housing the Boeing B-17 Flying Fortresses of the 390th Bomb Group, a vast amount of material has been carefully gathered together to present a history of the base, the unit and of the activities of the 3rd Air Division. Many artefacts have been collected from local crash sites, including a Merlin engine. A DC-3 arrived in March 1995 and restoration is underway.

Aircraft exhibit:

☐ N4565L	Douglas DC-3-201A	US '39

Nearby:
Mechanical Music Museum, Cotton, *16 miles*.
Museum of East Anglia Life, Stowmarket, *20 miles*.
Norfolk & Suffolk Aviation Museum, *18 miles – see page 16*.
100th Bomb Group Museum, *14 miles – see opposite*.
Woodbridge Tide Mill & Sutton Hoo, *8 miles*.
See overleaf.

The restored control tower at Parham looks out on the former 390th BG's dispersals. Ken Ellis

ALSO
IN EAST ANGLIA

AIRSHIP HERITAGE TRUST

A display room, located within RAF Cardington, south of Bedford. Fascinating display on the history of airships, especially relating to Cardington where the huge airship sheds still stand. The Trust also maintains a display at the Shuttleworth Collection – see page 19. Access to the display room at Cardington by prior arrangement only. Send SAE to G/C P A Garth, 5 Orchard Lane, Brampton, Huntingdon, Cambridgeshire, PE1 8TF.

BASSINGBOURNE TOWER MUSEUM

Within Allenbrooke Barracks, Bassingbourne, Cambridgeshire. Restored watch tower devoted in great detail to the history of the former airfield, including the 91st Bomb Group and the RAF's 11 OTU and 231 OCU, operated by the East Anglian

Aviation Society. Visits by prior arrangement only. Send SAE to M Reynolds, 8 Pringle Lane, Northborough, Peterborough, Cambridgeshire, PE6 9BW.

BLYTH VALLEY AVIATION COLLECTION

Expanding collection of aircraft and artefacts at Walpole, Suffolk (including six nose sections and EE Lightning F.3 XR718) holding occasional open days but also viewable by prior arrangement. Send SAE to Cliff Aldred, 'Vulcan's End', Mells Road, Walpole, Halesworth, Suffolk, IP19 0PL.

VULCAN RESTORATION TRUST

Look after the static Avro Vulcan B.2 XL426 at Southend Airport, Essex. Supporters club and regular magazine. Occasional open days, when the airframe goes 'live', otherwise visits by prior arrangement. Contact: Ricky Clarkson, 39 Breakspears Drive, St Pauls Cray, Orpington, Kent, BR5 2RX.

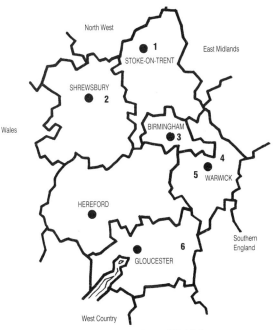

HEART OF ENGLAND
Gloucestershire, Hereford & Worcester, Shropshire, Staffordshire,
Warwickshire and the West Midlands.

1 Stoke-on-Trent City Museum &
   Art Gallery
2 Aerospace Museum
3 Birmingham Museum of
   Science & Industry
4 Midland Air Museum
5 Wellesbourne Wartime
   Museum
6 Wellington Museum & Art
   Gallery

Heart of England Tourist Board
Woodside, Larkhill Road, Worcester, WR5 2EF
Tel: 01905 763436 Fax: 01905 763450

AEROSPACE MUSEUM
Cosford, Shropshire

Address: Cosford, Shifnal, Shropshire, TF11 8UP.
Telephone: 01902 374112 or '374872, Fax 01902 374813.
Where: On the A41 south east of Shifnal, signed off Junction 3, M54.
Open: Daily 10am to 5pm with the exception of Xmas and New Year, last admission 4pm.
By bus: Services to Albrighton from Wolverhampton and Telford.
By rail: Cosford Halt – walking distance.
Tourist: Ironbridge 01952 432166, Fax 01952 432204. Telford 01952 291370, Fax 01952 291723.
Admission: Adult £4.20, OAP £3.10, Child £2.40, Family Ticket £11.00.
Facilities: Toilets/Parking/Cafe/Shop/Disabled/All/Changes/Brochure.

What began as an 'out-station' of the RAF Museum is now an international size and status collection in

Cosford's beautifully restored Flying Flea. Ken Ellis

its own right. In fact, the Aerospace Museum is really four-in-one museums with the transport aircraft collection including the British Airways exhibits; the world-renowned missile collection; the research and development aircraft collection and the warplane collection. There are hundreds of support items, including a growing engine collection. Set in 25 acres within RAF Cosford – the museum affords views of activity on the airfield – there are two huge display halls and an impressive open air static park, dominated by the transport collection including the Short Belfast, the largest aircraft in regular museum care in Great Britain. Airliner exhibits are opened to the public on various occasions. The museum stages regular special events and exhibitions, including a Flight Activities week during the autumn school half-term where visitors can sit in a variety of aircraft; an annual large model aircraft rally and the annual open day and airshow.

Aircraft exhibits:

☐	G-AEEH	Mignet HM.14 Flying Flea	Fr '36
☐	'G-AFAP'	CASA 352L (Ju 52) (T2B-272)	Gr c52
☐	G-AIZE	Fairchild Argus II	§ US '43
☐	'G-AJOV'	Westland Dragonfly HR.3 (WP495)	US '52
☐	G-AMOG	Vickers Viscount 701	'53

☐	G-AOVF	Bristol Britannia 312F	'58
☐	G-APAS	DH Comet 1XB	'53
☐	G-APFJ	Boeing 707-436	US '59
☐	G-ARPH	HS Trident 1C	'64
☐	G-ARVM	Vickers VC-10 Srs 1101	'63
☐	G-AVMO	BAC 111-510ED	'67
☐	'D3419'	Sopwith Camel replica (BAPC.59)	'17
☐	K4972	Hawker Hart Trainer	'35
☐	'K7271'	Hawker Fury II replica (BAPC.148)	§ '31
☐	DG202/G	Gloster F.9/40 Meteor	'42
☐	HS503	Fairey Swordfish IV (BAPC.108)	§ '44
☐	'KG374'	Douglas Dakota IV (KN645) [YS]	US '44
☐	'KL216'	Republic P-47D Thunderbolt (13064) [RS-L]	US '45
☐	KN751	Consolidated Liberator VI	US '45
☐	RF398	Avro Lincoln B.2	'45
☐	RW393	Supermarine Spitfire XVI [XT-A]	'45
☐	TA639	DH Mosquito TT.35	'45
☐	TG511	HP Hastings T.5	'48
☐	TS798	Avro York C.1	'45
☐	TX214	Avro Anson C.19	'46
☐	VP952	DH Devon C.2/2	'47
	VX461	DH Vampire FB.5	§ '48
☐	VX573	Vickers Valetta C.3	§ '49
☐	WA634	Gloster Meteor T.7 ejection seat test-bed	'49
☐	WD931	EE Canberra B.2 nose	'51
☐	WE600	Auster C4 'Antarctic'	'51
☐	WE982	Slingsby Prefect TX.1	'50
☐	WG760	EE P.1A	'54
☐	WG768	Short SB.5	'52
☐	WG777	Fairey FD-2	'56
☐	WK935	Gloster Meteor F.8 prone pilot test-bed	'53
☐	WL679	Vickers Varsity T.1	'53
☐	WL732	BP Sea Balliol T.21	'54
☐	WP912	DHC Chipmunk T.10	'52
☐	WS843	Gloster Meteor NF.14 [Y]	§ '54
☐	WV562	Percival Provost T.1 [P-C]	'54
☐	WV746	Percival Pembroke C.1	'55
☐	WZ744	Avro 707C	'53
☐	XA564	Gloster Javelin FAW.1	'55
☐	XA893	Avro Vulcan B.1 nose	'56
☐	XD145	SARO SR.53	'56
☐	XD674	Hunting Jet Provost T.1	'54

☐	XF785	Bristol 173 Srs 1	§ '52
☐	XF926	Bristol T.188	'63
☐	XG337	EE Lightning F.1	'59
☐	XH171	EE Canberra PR.9 [U]	'58
☐	XH672	HP Victor K.2	'60
☐	XJ918	Bristol Sycamore HR.14	'56
☐	XK724	Folland Gnat F.1	'56
☐	XL703	SAL Pioneer CC.1	'56
☐	XL993	SAL Twin Pioneer CC.1	'58
☐	XM555	SARO Skeeter AOP.12	§ '60
☐	XM598	Avro Vulcan B.2	'63
☐	XN714	Hunting 126	'63
☐	XP299	Westland Whirlwind HAR.10	US '61
☐	XP411	AW Argosy C.1	'62
☐	XR220	BAC TSR-2	'65
☐	XR371	Short Belfast C.1	'65
☐	XR977	Folland Gnat T.1	'66
☐	XS639	HS Andover E.3A	'66
☐	XV591	McDD Phantom FG.1 nose	US '70
☐	XW547	HS Buccaneer S.2B	'72
☐	A-515	FMA Pucara (ZD485)	Arg c76
☐	J-1704	DH Venom FB.4	c55
☐	L-866	Consolidated PBY-6A Catalina	US '45
☐	204	Lockheed SP-2H Neptune	US '53
☐	5439	Mitsubishi Ki 46-III 'Dinah'	Ja '45
☐	6130	Lockheed Ventura II	US '42
☐	'6771'	Republic F-84F Thunderstreak [FU-6]	US '52
☐	112372	Messerschmitt Me 262A-2a	Gr '44
☐	191614	Messerschmitt Me 163B-1a Komet	Gr '44
☐	420430	Messerschmitt Me 410A-1-U2 Hornisse [3U+CC]	Gr '43
☐	475081	Fieseler Fi 156C-7 Storch	Gr '42
☐	–	Fieseler Fi 103 (V-1) flying-bomb (BAPC.94)	Gr c44
☐	–	Focke-Achgelis Fa 330A-1 rotorkite	Gr c44
☐	–	Hawker P.1121 fuselage	§ '58
☐	–	Kawasaki Ki 100-1b (BAPC.83)	Ja '45
☐	–	Yokosuka MXY7 Ohka 11 (BAPC.99) suicide weapon	Ja c45

Nearby:

Ironbridge Gorge Industrial Museums, *8 miles.*
Severn Valley Railway, *16 miles.*

BIRMINGHAM MUSEUM OF SCIENCE AND INDUSTRY

Birmingham, West Midlands

Address: Newhall Street, Birmingham, B3 1RZ.
Telephone: 0121 2351661, Fax 0121 2339210.
Where: North of the junction of the A38, A456 and A457 in Birmingham city centre.
Open: Monday to Saturday 10am to 5pm and Sunday 12.30pm to 5pm.
By bus: Many bus routes pass the door or stop close by.
By rail: Birmingham New Street, walking distance.
Tourist: Birmingham 0121 6432514, Fax 0121 6161038. **Admission:** Free.
Facilities: Toilets/Cafe/Shop/Disabled/Kids/All/ Brochure.

As well as the Hurricane and Spitfire, the museum has a large number of artefacts relating to aviation, including a collection of aero engines. Extensive other exhibits and displays with a predominant transport and industrial theme.

Aircraft exhibits:

☐ 'P3395'	Hawker Hurricane IV (KX829) [JX-B]	'43
☐ ML427	V-S Spitfire IX [IS-T]	'44

Nearby:

Aston Transport Museum, *2 miles.*
Birmingham Bus Museum, *10 miles.*
Birmingham Railway Museum, *3 miles.*
Midland Air Museum, *20 miles – see opposite.*
National Motorcycle Museum, *10 miles.*

Top: **General view of Cosford's main exhibition hangar.**
Aerospace Museum
Middle: **Short SB.5 WG768, aerodynamic research aircraft for the EE Lightning, 1952.** MAP
Bottom: **DH Mosquito TA639 with Avro Lincoln RF398 behind.** Ken Ellis

MIDLAND AIR MUSEUM AND AEROSPACE EDUCATION CENTRE

Coventry Airport, Warwickshire

Address: Baginton, Coventry, CV8 3AZ.
Telephone: 01203 301033 plus fax.
Where: Signed from the A45/A423 junction to the south west of Coventry city centre.
Open: Open daily (excluding Christmas) 10.30am to 5pm.
By bus: Metro Bus Service, T route.
By rail: Coventry 3 miles.
Tourist: Coventry 01203 832303 or '832304, Fax 01203 832370.
Admission: Adult £3, OAP £2.25, Child £2, Family ticket £8.50.
Facilities: Toilets/Parking/Cafe/Shop/Disabled/ All/Changes/Brochure.

Overlooking Coventry airport and offering good views of the activity there, the museum provides an 'then' to the airport's 'now'. Inside the excellent display hall – the Frank Whittle Jet Heritage centre – can be found aircraft tracing the history of the jet engine and a vivid display charting the development of the turbojet and Whittle's key role. The 'Wings over Coventry' display highlights the area's contribution to the development of aviation through the many companies that have built aircraft locally. The static aircraft park has over 25 exhibits, with some available for internal inspection on special days. Construction of a workshop using an original Robin hangar is underway. The museum has developed and aerospace education centre in association with local colleges and schools. Annual 'Wings and Wheels' gala day and other special events are staged.

Aircraft exhibits:

☐ G-EBJG	Parnall Pixie III ultralight	§ '26
☐ G-ABOI	Wheeler Slymph ultralight	§ '31
☐ G-AEGV	Mignet HM.14 Flying Flea	§ Fr '36

☐ G-ALCU	DH Dove 2	'47
☐ G-APJJ	Fairey Ultra Light helicopter	'58
☐ G-APRL	AW Argosy 101	'59
☐ G-APWN	Westland Whirlwind Srs 3	US '59
☐ G-ARYB	HS.125 Srs 1	'62
☐ G-MJWH	Chargus Vortex 120 hang glider	'83
☐ BGA.804	Slingsby Cadet TX.1 (VM589)	§ '48
☐ 'A7317'	Sopwith Pup replica (BAPC.179)	'17
☐ EE531	Gloster Meteor F.4	'46
☐ VF301	DH Vampire F.1 [RAL-G]	'46
☐ VM325	Avro Anson C.19	§ '47
☐ VS623	Percival Prentice T.1 (G-AOKZ)	'49
☐ VT935	BP 111A delta research aircraft	'50
☐ VZ477	Gloster Meteor F.8 nose	'49
☐ WF922	EE Canberra PR.3	'53
☐ WS838	Gloster Meteor NF.14	'54
☐ WV797	Hawker Sea Hawk FGA.6	'54
☐ XA508	Fairey Gannet T.2 [627-GN]	'54
☐ XA699	Gloster Javelin FAW.5	'57
☐ XD626	DH Vampire T.11	'54
☐ XE855	DH Vampire T.11 nose	§ '54
☐ XF382	Hawker Hunter F.6A [15]	'55
☐ XJ579	DH Sea Vixen FAW.2 nose	'58
☐ XK741	Folland Gnat F.1 fuselage	'55
☐ XK907	Westland Whirlwind HAS.7 cockpit	US '57
☐ XL360	Avro Vulcan B.2	'62
☐ XN685	DH Sea Vixen FAW.2	'61
☐ XR771	EE Lightning F.6 [BM]	'66
☐ ZF598	EE Lightning T.55	'67
☐ E-425	Hawker Hunter F.51	'56

☐ R-756	Lockheed F-104G Starfighter	US c62
☐ 70	Dassault Mystère IVA	Fr '55
☐ 17473	Lockheed T-33A 'T-Bird'	US '51
☐ 24535	Kaman HH-43B Huskie	US '62
☐ 28368	Flettner Fl 282V Kolibri frame	Gr '44
☐ 29640	SAAB J29F	Sw '52
☐ 37699	McDD F-4C Phantom	US '63
☐ 70270	Mc Donnell F-101B Voodoo cockpit	US '57
☐ 51-4419	Lockheed T-33A 'T-Bird'	US '51
☐ 54-2174	NA F-100D Super Sabre	US '54
☐ 56-0312	McDonnell F-101B Voodoo	US '56
☐ 58-2062	DHC U-6A Beaver	Can '58
☐ 63-7414	McDD F-4C Phantom	US '63
☐ –	Bristol Beaufighter cockpit	c43
☐ –	Crossley Tom Thumb homebuild (BAPC.32)	§ '37
☐ –	Druine Turbulent (BAPC.126)	c64
☐ –	Hawker Hurricane replica (BAPC.68)	§ '40
☐ –	Humber Monoplane replica (BAPC.9)	'12

Nearby:

Birmingham Museum of Science and Industry,
20 miles – see page 29.

Bosworth Battlefield and Market Bosworth Light
Railway, *20 miles.*

City of Coventry (and Cathedral), *3 miles.*

Heritage Motor Museum, Gaydon, *14 miles.*

Percy Pilcher Museum, *14 miles – see page 55.*

Wellesbourne Wartime Museum, *14 miles –
see page 32..*

'Edna', Midland Air Museum's Argosy 101 freighter. Ken Ellis

Top: **A view of the aircraft park, Dassault Mystère in the foreground.**

Middle: **The Sopwith Pup replica forms a part of the 'Wings over Coventry' exhbition.** Both Ken Ellis

Bottom: **The Boulton Paul 111A delta wing research aircraft, built at Wolverhampton in 1950.** Author's collection

STOKE-ON-TRENT CITY MUSEUM AND ART GALLERY

Stoke-on-Trent, Staffordshire

Address: Bethesda St, Hanley, Stoke, ST13DW.
Telephone: 01782 202173, Fax 01782 205033.
Where: In Bethesda Street, off Broad Street, Hanley. Use junction 15 from M6.
Open: Daily 10.30am to 5pm Monday to Saturday and Sundays 2pm to 5pm.
By bus: Hanley bus and coach station close to.
By rail: Stoke-on-Trent 2 miles.
Tourist: Stoke 01782 284600.
Admission: Free.
Facilities: Toilets/Parking/Cafe/Shop/Disabled/All/Changes/Brochure.

Reginald J Mitchell, the designer of the Spitfire, was born in Stoke-on-Trent and with the Spitfire as a centre-piece, the museum has a display devoted to one of its famous sons. Other subjects on exhibition include natural history, archaeology, social history, fine art, decorative art and an incredible ceramics collection. Special events organised – details from the museum.

Aircraft exhibit:

☐ RW388   Supermarine Spitfire XVI [U4-U]   '45

Also: The museum is part of the Potteries Heritage Trail that takes in 20 venues all linked by tourist 'brown signs' and a detailed leaflet. Also an hourly minibus link – The China Service – connecting up Stoke's major china attractions. (Leaflet and more details available from the Stoke-on-Trent TIC.)

Nearby:
Alton Towers, *14 miles.*
Brindley Water Mill, Leek, *10 miles.*
Chatterly Whitfield Mining Museum, *4 miles.*
Cheddleton Railway Centre, *8 miles.*
Foxfield Steam Railway, *6 miles.*
Jodrell Bank Radio Telescope, *16 miles.*

WELLESBOURNE WARTIME MUSEUM

Wellesbourne Mountford, Warwickshire

Address: Alan Barker, 15 Mountbatten Avenue, Kenilworth, Warks, CV8 2PY.
Telephone: 01926 55031.
Where: South of Wellesbourne Mountford village, follow signs to the airfield.
Open: Every Sunday 10am to 4pm and Bank Holidays, same times.
By rail: Stratford-upon-Avon 4 miles.
Tourist: Stratford-upon-Avon 01789 293127, Fax 01789 295262.
Admission: Adult £1, Child 50p.
Facilities: Disabled/All/Changes/Brochure.

Fascinating museum with many of the displays inside the airfield's former underground battle headquarters. Displays are largely devoted to the history of Wellesbourne Mountford airfield, the home of 22 OTU during the Second World War. Excellent reconstructions include the cockpit of a Spitfire including working gun sight and the turret area from a Blenheim. Both the Vampire and the Sea Vixen are available for internal inspection and work in progress on the Provost is viewable. The airfield is an active general aviation centre and the comings and goings can be seen to advantage from the museum.

Aircraft exhibits:

☐ WV679   Percival Provost T.1 [O-J]   '54
☐ XJ575   DH Sea Vixen FAW.2 nose   '59
☐ XK590   DH Vampire T.11 [V]   '56

Nearby:
City of Coventry, *16 miles.*
Heritage Motor Museum, Gaydon, *6 miles.*
Midland Air Museum, *14 miles – see page 29.*
Stratford-upon-Avon, *3 miles.*
Warwick Castle, *6 miles.*
Wellington Museum, *14 miles – see page 34.*

Above: **Stoke's Spitfire is moved into position, 1985**. Alan Curry

Above: **Wellesbourne's restored Vampire T.11 and 'hangar-ette'.**
Below: **Gloster Javelin FAW.9 XH903 under restoration at Hucclecote, see overleaf.** Both Ken Ellis

WELLINGTON MUSEUM AND AVIATION GALLERY

Moreton-in-the-Marsh, Gloucestershire

Address: British School House, Moreton-in-the-Marsh, Glos, GL56 0BG.
Telephone: 01608 560323.
Where: On the A44 to the west of the village of Moreton-in-the-Marsh.
Open: 10am to 12.30am and 2pm to 5.30pm daily.
By bus: On Worcester-London route and local services to Cheltenham.
By rail: Moreton-in-the-Marsh, walking distance.
Tourist: Chipping Camden* 01386 840101. Stow-on-the-Wold 01451 831082. Fax 01451 870083.
Admission: Adult £1. Child 50p.
Facilities: Toilets/Parking/Shop/Disabled*/All/Changes/Brochure.

A museum with a considerable difference. Gerry Tyack's excellent aviation art and print gallery has expanded to take on a much greater role, not only telling via photographs and artefacts the stories behind some of the paintings and prints on show but including the history of the former local airfield, which was home to 21 OTU and their Wellingtons. Substantial remains from a former 20 OTU Wellington which crashed in Scotland in October 1940 are also held.

Aircraft exhibit:

☐ L7775   Vickers Wellington I sections   '39

Nearby:

Gloucestershire and Warwickshire Railway, *12 miles.*
Heritage Motor Museum, Gaydon, *16 miles.*
Stratford-upon-Avon, *16 miles.*
Wellesbourne Wartime Museum, 14 miles – *see page 32.*

ALSO IN THE HEART OF ENGLAND

The **COTSWOLD AIRCRAFT RESTORATION GROUP**, have a workshop within RAF Innsworth, near Cheltenham, with work on several projects currently underway, including an Auster AOP.9, and numerous sub assemblies for other restoration projects. Visits by prior arrangement only. Send SAE to: Steve Thompson, 'Kia-Ora', Risbury, Leominster, Herefordshire, HR6 0NQ.

GLOUCESTERSHIRE AVIATION COLLECTION, is an expanding collection working towards the establishment of a permanent museum at Hucclecote, devoted to the production of local aircraft and the aviation history of the region. Aircraft under restoration on site include a Meteor T.7, Javelin FAW.9, Sea Venom FAW.22 and a Harrier T.2 cockpit. Gloster Gamecock replica underway. Sunday openings during 1995, but GAC plan to open on a more regular basis during 1996. Send SAE to : GAC, Unit 2B, Gloucester Trading Estate, Hucclecote, Gloucester GL3 4AA or telephone 01242 515533 or '577240.

JET AIRCRAFT PRESERVATION GROUP are hard at work on a number of projects at Long Marston airfield, Warwickshire. Included in the collection are Vampire T.11, Jet Provost T.4 and a Hunter composite that will be finished as a FR.10. Visitors are welcome at weekends when JAPG members are at work on the aircraft. Other times by arrangement, send SAE to : Stewart Holder, 62 Avon Street, Evesham, Worcester, WR11 4LG.

GREATER LONDON

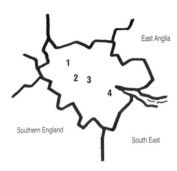

East Anglia

1
2 3
4

Southern England

South East

1 Royal Air Force Museum
2 Science Museum
3 Imperial War Museum
4 Museum of Artillery

London Tourist Board,
26 Grosvenor Gardens, London, SW1W 0DU
Tel: 0171 7303450 Fax: 0171 7309367

Visitorcall is a service providing pre-recorded information on a wide range of subjects,
dial 0891 505 plus the following numbers for information: **440** What's on in London this week;
462 Museums; **465** Popular attractions; **467** Greenwich and Military Museums;
468 Famous Houses and Gardens – and many more, details from the LTB.

IMPERIAL WAR MUSEUM
South Lambeth

Address: Lambeth Road, London, SE1 6HZ.
Telephone: 0171 416 5320, Fax 0171 416 5374.
Where: South east of Waterloo Station, off Kenington Road (the A23).
Open: Open 10am to 6pm daily. Closed 24-26th December.
By bus: Many services.
By rail: Underground, Lambeth North and Elephant & Castle; Mainline Waterloo.
Tourist: London 0171 7303450, Fax 0171 7309367.
Admission: Adult £4.10, Cons £3.10, Child £2.05, Family ticket £11.
Facilities: Toilets/Cafe/Shop/Disabled/All/Changes/Brochure.

While the vast majority of the Imperial War Museum's aircraft collection is at Duxford (see under East Anglia), aviation is far from absent in the famous Lambeth premises. The aviation galleries were given a major refurbishment some years ago and many of the airframes are posed in dramatic 'flying trim'. The remainder of the museum holds a wealth of material and all aspects of 20th century warfare with many 'inter-active' displays and vibrant presentations. Special events and exhibitions are staged throughout the year, including presentations aimed specifically at children. There is an excellent cinema showing archive films and other footage.

Aircraft exhibits:

☐ 2699	RAF BE.2c	'16
☐ N6812	Sopwith Camel 2F1	'18
☐ R6915	Supermarine Spitfire I	'40
☐ DV372	Avro Lancaster I nose	'43
☐ PN323	HP Halifax A.VII nose	'45
☐ 120235	Heinkel He 162A-1	Gr '45
☐ 733682	Focke-Wulf FW 190A-8	Gr c43
☐ '472258'	NA P-51D Mustang (44-73979) [WZ-I]	US '44
☐ –	Fieseler Fi 103 (V-1) flying-bomb (BAPC.198)	Gr '45
☐ –	Mitsubishi A6M 'Zero' cockpit	Ja c44

Lt Culley's Camel downed Zeppelin L.53 on 11th August 1918. Bill Hale

Also:
There are two other Imperial War Museum sites in London. **HMS** *Belfast* at Morgan's Lane (London Bridge or Tower Hill Underground), more details on 0171 407 6434 and the **Cabinet War Rooms** in King Charles Street (Westminster or St James's Park Underground), more details on 0171 930 6961.

Lambeth's Ruston-built BE.2c after restoration at Duxford, 1984. Ken Ellis

Nearby:
Brooklands Museum, *16 miles – see page 70.*
Lambeth Palace, *1 mile.*
Mosquito Aircraft Museum, *20 miles – see page 14.*
Museum of Artillery, *8 miles – see below.*
RAF Museum, *9 miles – see page 38.*
Science Museum, *5 miles – see page 42.*
Shoreham Aircraft Preservation Society, *16 miles – see page 78.*
Westminster, *2 miles.*

MUSEUM OF ARTILLERY
Woolwich

Address: The Old Royal Military Academy, Woolwich, London, SE18 4JJ.
Telephone: 0181 3165402, Fax 0181 7815929.
Where: Within the Royal Artillery Institution at The Rotunda, off the A206.
Open: Open Monday to Friday and 1pm to 4pm. Closed Bank Holidays and Public Holidays.
By bus: Several bus services.
By rail: Woolwich Arsenal, walking distance.
Tourist: Greenwich, 0181 858 6376.
Facilities: Toilets/Parking/Shop/Disabled*/ All/Brochure. **Admission:** Free.

Telling the story of artillery from the earliest times to the latest laser and satellite guided weaponry the museum includes within its collection an Auster AOP.9 as an example of 'eyes for the guns'.

Aircraft exhibit:
☐ XR271　Auster AOP.9　'62

Nearby:
Imperial War Museum, *8 miles, see opposite.*
Maritime Trust, Greenwich and Southwark, *3 miles.*
RAF Museum, *14 miles – see page 38.*
Science Museum, *13 miles – see page 42.*
Shoreham Aircraft Preservation Society, *16 miles – see page 78.*

ROYAL AIR FORCE MUSEUM

Hendon

Address: Hendon, London, NW9 5LL.
Telephone: 0181 2052266, Event hotline 081 205 9191, Fax 0181 2008044.
Where: On Grahame Park Way, signposted from the end of the M1.
Open: 10am to 6pm all week, with the exception of Christmas and New Year.
By bus: No 303 Mill Hill–Colindale–Edgware. Thameslink, Mill Hill.
By rail: Colindale Underground, Northern Line.
Tourist: London 0171 7303450, Fax 0171 7309367.
Admission: Adult £5.20, Cons £2.60.
Facilities: Toilets/Parking/Cafe/Shop/Disabled/ Kids/All/Changes/Brochure.

The site is essentially three museums rolled into one, the RAF Museum itself, the Bomber hall and the Battle of Britain Experience, all located on the former and historic Hendon airfield. As well as the aircraft halls there are many galleries – including

'RAF 2000' with a wide-screen presentation of the Eurofighter, always an art or photograph exhibition, 'Plane and Simple' demonstrations on the theory of flight, a free cinema showing classic films and other footage, Tornado flight simulator, TriStar flight deck and a 'Touch and Try' Jet Provost cockpit. The Sunderland flying-boat is now equipped with a walkway though its cavernous fuselage. The acclaimed Battle of Britain Experience includes the use of excellent dioramas and 'talking' mannequins that take the visitor through the Blitz and the aerial battles from the perspective of the 'man in the street'. The museum has a vigorous policy of staging special events and exhibitions including the Flight Activities week for younger including workshops for youngsters, simulators and pleasure flying. Note that the RAF Museum has many more aircraft on charge than are listed below, these are on loan to other musuems (including the bulk of the aircraft at Manchester), under restoration or in store. See also Aerospace Museum Cosford, Heart of England, which is an RAF Museum site.

Bombers through the ages; Sopwith Tabloid (1914) and Avro Vulcan (1961). Alan Curry

Nearby:
Blake Hall, *20 miles – see page 8.*
Brooklands Museum, *20 miles – see page 70.*
Central London, *8 miles.*
Hatfield House, *20 miles.*
Imperial War Museum, *10 miles – see page 36..*

Mosquito Aircraft Museum, *10 miles –*
see page 14.
North Weald Airfield Museum, *20 miles –*
see page 17.
Science Museum, *8 miles – see page 42.*

Above: **Hendon's Stranraer in civilian hands, Canada, 1951.** CAHS

Below: **View of part of the main hall at Hendon. Note the 'Belfast Truss' construction of the World War One period hangars.** RAF Museum

Aircraft exhibits:

	Reg/No.	Type	Origin/Date
☐	G-EBMB	Hawker Cygnet	'24
☐	164	Bleriot XI (BAPC.106)	Fr c09
☐	'168'	Sopwith Tabloid replica (G-BFDE)	'14
☐	433	Bleriot XXVII (BAPC.107)	Fr '12
☐	'687'	RAF BE.2b replica (BAPC.181)	'14
☐	'2345'	Vickers Gunbus replica (G-ATVP)	'14
☐	'3066'	Caudron G.III	Fr c16
☐	A301	Morane BB fuselage frame	Fr '15
☐	'E449'	Avro 504K	c17
☐	F938	RAF SE.5A (G-EBIC)	'18
☐	'A8226'	Sopwith 1½ Strutter replica (G-BIDW)	'16
☐	'C4994'	Bristol M.1C replica (G-BLWM)	'17
☐	'E2466'	Bristol F.2b Fighter (BAPC.165)	'18
☐	F1010	Airco DH.9A	'18
☐	F6314	Sopwith Camel F.1	c17
☐	'F8614'	Vickers Vimy replica (G-AWAU)	'18
☐	'J9941'	Hawker Hart (G-ABMR)	'31
☐	K4232	Avro Rota I (Cierva C.30A)	'34
☐	K6035	Westland Wallace II fuselage	'35
☐	K8042	Gloster Gladiator II	'37
☐	K9942	Sup Spitfire IA [SD-V]	'39
☐	L5343	Fairey Battle I [VO-S]	'39
☐	'L8756'	Bristol Bolingbroke IVT (10001) [XD-E]	'42
☐	N1671	BP Defiant I [EW-D]	'40
☐	'N5182'	Sopwith Pup replica (G-APUP)	'17
☐	N5628	Gloster Gladiator II fuselage	'39
☐	N5912	Sopwith Triplane	'17
☐	N9899	Supermarine Southampton I fuselage	'25
☐	P2617	Hawker Hurricane I [AF-F]	'40
☐	P3175	Hawker Hurricane I wreck	'40
☐	R5868	Avro Lancaster I [PO-S]	'42
☐	R9125	Westland Lysander III [LX-L]	'40
☐	T6296	DH Tiger Moth II	'41
☐	W1048	HP Halifax II [TL-S]	'42
☐	X4590	Supermarine Spitfire I [PR-F]	'40
☐	Z7197	Percival Proctor III	'40
☐	'BE421'	Hawker Hurricane replica (BAPC.205) [XP-G]	'41
☐	'DD931'	Bristol Beaufort VIII [L]	'42
☐	FE905	NA Harvard IIB	US '43
☐	'FX760'	Cutiss Kittyhawk IV [GA-?]	US '43
☐	KK995	Sikorsky Hoverfly I [E]	'44
☐	MF628	Vickers Wellington T.10	'44
☐	'MH486'	Sup Spitfire replica (BAPC.206) [FF-A]	'43
☐	ML824	Short Sunderland V [NS-Z]	'44
☐	MN235	Hawker Typhoon IB	'43
☐	MP425	Airspeed Oxford I	'43
☐	PK724	Supermarine Spitfire F.24	'46
☐	'PR536'	Hawker Tempest II (HA457) [OQ-H]	'45
☐	RD253	Bristol Beaufighter TF.10	'44
☐	TJ138	DH Mosquito TT.35 [VO-L]	'45
☐	VT812	DH Vampire F.3 [N]	'47
☐	WE139	EE Canberra PR.3	'53
☐	WH301	Gloster Meteor F.8	'51
☐	WZ791	Slingsby Grasshopper TX.1	'58
☐	XB812	NA Sabre F.4 [U]	US '53
☐	XD818	Vickers Valiant BK.1	'56
☐	XG154	Hawker Hunter FGA.9	'57
☐	XG474	Bristol Belvedere HC.1 [O]	'62
☐	XL318	Avro Vulcan B.2	'61
☐	XM463	Hunting Jet Provost T.3A fuselage [38]	'60
☐	XS925	EE Lightning F.6 [BA]	'67
☐	XV424	McDD Phantom FGR.2 [I]	'69
☐	XW323	BAC Jet Provost T.5A [86]	'70
☐	XX946	Panavia Tornado UK prototype	'74
☐	XZ997	HS Harrier GR.3 [V]	'82
☐	A2-4	Supermarine Seagull V	'37
☐	A16-199	Lockheed Hudson IIIA (G-BEOX) [SF-R]	US '41
☐	HD-75	Hanriot HD.1	Fr '17
☐	MM5701	Fiat CR-42 [13-95]	It '40
☐	920	Supermarine Stranraer [QN]	'40
☐	1120	MiG MiG-15bis 'Fagot'	c55
☐	4101	Messerschmitt Bf 109E-3 [12]	Gr '40
☐	'34037'	NA TB-25N Mitchell (N9115Z)	US '44
☐	120227	Heinkel He 162A-2	Gr '45
☐	360043	Junkers Ju 88R-1 [D5+EV]	Gr c42
☐	'413573'	NA P-51D Mustang (N6526D) [B6-K]	US '44
☐	494083	Junkers Ju 87D-3 [RI+JK]	Gr c40
☐	584219	Focke-Wulf Fw 190F-8/U1 [38]	Gr c42
☐	701	Heinkel He 111H-23 [NT+SL]	Gr '42
☐	730301	Me Bf 110G-4/R6 [D5+RL]	Gr c42
☐	44-83868	Boeing B-17G Flying Fortress [N]	US '44
☐	–	Clarke TWK hang glider (BAPC.100)	'10
☐	–	Fieseler Fi 103 (V-1) (BAPC.92)	Gr c45
☐	–	Hawker Hind (Afghan) (BAPC.82)	c37
☐	–	'Nulli Secundus' airship gondola	'07

Top: **Fairey Battle I L5343, salvaged from Iceland where it had force landed on 13th September 1940.**
Above: **The Battle of Britain Hall, nearest the camera is the Messerschmitt Bf 110G-4/R6 night fighter.**
Both Alan Curry

SCIENCE MUSEUM
South Kensington

Address: South Kensington, London SW7 2DD.
Telephone: 071 9388080 or '9388008,
Fax 071 9388112.
Where: Exhibition Road, off Cromwell Road (A4).
Open: Open daily 10am to 6pm.
By bus: Variety of service.
By rail: South Kensington Underground.
Tourist: London 0171 7303450, Fax 0171
7309367.
Admission: Adult £4.50, Child/cons £2.40.
Facilities: Toilets/Cafe/Shop/Disabled/Kids/All/
Changes/Brochure.

Recently restyled and refurbished under the heading 'Flight' the museum's aeronautical gallery is an impressive sight with its overhead walkways, 'stacks' of aero engines and walk-around and through exhibits. All this before the visitor takes in the historic importance of the aircraft exhibits on view, including the first British powered aircraft to fly (the Roe), the first to fly the Atlantic non-stop (the Vimy) and the first British jet aircraft, the Gloster E.28/39). On one wall is a cross section from a scrapped Boeing 747 'Jumbo' jet, putting that world beating aircraft into awesome proportion. Alongside the 'Flight' gallery is 'Flight Lab' where the principals of flight can be explored in a 'hands-on' manner, including a Cessna 150 that youngsters can 'fly'. The remainder of the museum is just as absorbing taking in transport, technology and science. Regular special exhibitions and displays are staged.

Aircraft exhibits:

☐ G-EBIB	RAF SE.5A	'18
☐ G-AAAH	DH Moth	'28
☐ G-ANAV	DH Comet 1A	'52
☐ G-ASSM	HS.125-1-522	'64
☐ G-ATTN	Piccard hot air balloon	§ Sws '66
☐ G-AWAW	Cessna F.150F	US '66
☐ G-AZPH	Pitts S-1S	US '70
☐ G-BBGN	Cameron A-375 balloon gondola	§ '73
☐ DFY	Schempp-Hirth Standard Cirrus glider	Gr '73
☐ OO-BFH	Piccard Gas balloon gondola	§ Sws '32

Left: **View of the Science Museum's 'Flight' gallery.** Science Museum
Top: **Schneider Trophy holder, Boothman's S.6B at Calshot, September 1931.** Digital
Below: **Moment of truth, A V Roe airborne in his Triplane, 3rd July 1909 to become the first Britain to fly in a British built *and* propelled aircraft.** Avro International

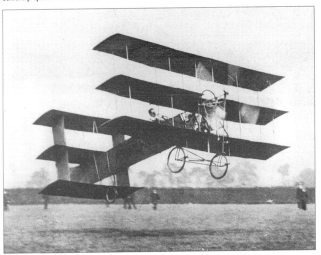

☐	304	Cody Biplane (BAPC.62)	'12
☐	J8067	Westland Pterodactyl I	'28
☐	L1592	Hawker Hurricane I [KW-Z]	'38
☐	P9444	Supermarine Spitfire IA [RN-D]	'40
☐	S1595	Supermarine S.6B	'31
☐	W4041/G	Gloster E.28/39	'41
☐	AP507	Cierva C.30A (Avro 671) [KX-P]	Sp '34
☐	KN448	Douglas Dakota IV nose	US '44
☐	XN344	SARO Skeeter AOP.12	'60
☐	XP831	Hawker P.1127	'60
☐	210/15	Fokker E.III (BAPC.56)	Gr '15
☐	100509	Focke-Achgelis Fa 330A-1 rotorkite	§ '43
☐	191316	Messerschmitt Me 163B-1 Komet	Gr '43
☐	442795	Fieseler Fi 103 (V-1) flying-bomb	Gr '44
☐	–	Airship No 17 'Beta II' gondola	'10
☐	–	Antoinette VII (BAPC.55)	Fr '10
☐	–	JAP-Harding Monoplane (BAPC.54)	'10
☐	–	Lilienthal Standard hang glider replica (BAPC.124)	Gr 1895
☐		McCready Gossamer Albatross man-powered aircraft	§ US '86
☐	–	Roe Triplane Type I (BAPC.50)	'09
☐		Short Brothers Gas balloon basket	'09
☐	–	Vickers Vimy IV (BAPC.51)	'18
☐	–	Wright Flyer replica (BAPC.53)	US '03

Nearby:

Brooklands Museum, *16 miles – see page 70*.
Geological Museum next door.
Harrods, *1 mile*.
Mosquito Aircraft Museum, *20 miles – see page 14*.
Natural History Museum next door.
Imperial War Museum, *5 miles – see page 36*.
RAF Museum, *8 miles – see page 38*.
Shoreham Aircraft Preservation Society, *16 miles – see page 78*.
Victoria and Albert Museum next door.

Britain's first jet aircraft, the Gloster E.28/39 powered by a Whittle W.1 of just 860 pounds thrust first flew on 15th May 1941. Alan Curry

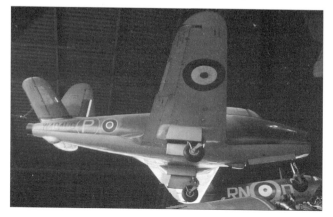

EAST MIDLANDS

Derbyshire, Leicestershire, Lincolnshire, Northamptonshire, Nottinghamshire

1 Bomber County Aviation
   Museum
2 Thorpe Camp Visitor Centre
3 Battle of Britain Memorial Flight
   Visitor Centre
4 Newark Air Museum

5 Lincolnshire Aviation Heritage
   Centre
6 Lincolnshire Aviation Heritage
   Trail – Cranwell, see text for
   others
7 Derby Industrial Museum

8 Aeropark & Visitor Centre
9 Snibston Discovery Park
10 Percy Pilcher Museum
11 'Carpetbaggers' & Northants
   Aviation Museums

East Midlands Tourist Board
Exchequergate, Lincoln, LN2 1PZ. Tel: 01522 531521 Fax: 01522 532501

AEROPARK
AND VISITORS CENTRE
East Midlands Airport, Leicestershire

Address: Castle Donington, Derby, DE7 2SA.
Telephone: 01332 852852 extension 3361.
Where: On the A453 south of Castle Donington, junction 23A M1.
Open: Aeropark open all year round from dawn to dusk, except for December 25 to January 1. Visitors Centre open Junie to September 10am to 6pm daily. October to May 10am to 5pm weekends, also open Easter week and Bank Holidays. Other times by appointment.
By bus: Services from Derby, Loughborough and Nottingham. By rail: Long Eaton, 5 miles.
Tourist: Derby 01332 255802.
Admission: Aeropark cars and minibuses £2, coaches £12 (inc occupants), Visitor Centre free.
Facilities: Toilets/Parking/Cafe/Shop/Disabled/ Kids/Brochure.

The Aeropark gives a commanding view of the activities of most of the airport and is amid the static aircraft park. These airframes are occasionally opened up to the public and the Varsity, for example, is ground run occasionally. The Visitors Centre contains a well presented history of the Airport and aviation in general and offers educational facilities.

Aircraft exhibits:

☐	G-BEOZ	AW Argosy 101	'60
☐	G-FRJB	Britten SA.1 Sheriff	'81
☐	VR-BEP	Westland Whirlwind Srs 3	US '56
☐	WH740	EE Canberra T.17 [X]	'53
☐	WL626	Vickers Varsity T.1 (G-BHDD) [P]	'56
☐	XL569	Hawker Hunter T.7 [80]	'58
☐	XM575	Avro Vulcan B.2 (G-BLMC)	'63
☐	XV350	HS Buccaneer S.2B	'67
☐	ZF588	EE Lightning F.53	'68

Nearby:
Bosworth Battlefield and Market Bosworth Light Railway, *14 miles.*
Brewery Museum, Burton-on-Trent, *14 miles.*
Derby Industrial Museum, *8 miles – see page 50.*
Donington Park Motor Racing Museum, *1 mile.*
Snibston Discovery Park, *10 miles – see page 56.*

Early in its career at East Midlands Airport, Vulcan B.2 XM575 carried its civil registration. Peter Green

BATTLE OF BRITAIN MEMORIAL FLIGHT VISITOR CENTRE

RAF Coningsby, Lincolnshire

Address: BBMF Visits, RAF Coningsby, Lincoln, LN4 4SY.

Telephone: 01526 344041.

Where: At RAF Coningsby, south of Coningsby village and signed off the A153.

Open: Monday to Friday except Bank Holidays 10am to 4.30pm with the last guided tour at 3.30pm. Note: although booking is not required to attend the Visitor Centre, it is advisable as it may be that the Flight in whole or in part are positioning to a show.

By bus: Services pass through Coningsby from Sleaford and Horncastle.

By rail: Sleaford 14 miles.

Tourist: Sleaford 01529 414294.

Admission: Adult £3, OAP/Children £1.50.

Facilities: Toilets/Parking/Shop/Disabled/All/ Changes/Brochure.

RAF Coningsby is the home of the Battle of Britain Memorial Flight, famed for their appearances at air events all over the country. The appeal of the Flight is such that in 1986, in a joint arrangement with Lincolnshire County Council, the centre was established so that people could see the aircraft of the Flight 'at home'. During the winter deep maintenance can be seen going on. In addition to the aircraft, there is an excellent historic display within the visitor centre itself. During the summer months, Flight aircraft may well be away and if visitors are intending to see a specific aircraft, it is important to telephone beforehand to check that it/they will be in attendance. The visitor centre is on the North Kesteven Airfield Trail, see page 51.

Aircraft exhibits:

☐ P7350	V-S Spitfire IIA ✈	[RN-S]	'40
☐ AB910	V-S Spitfire VB ✈	[AE]	'41
☐ LF363	Hawker Hurricane IIC		§ '44
☐ MK356	V-S Spitfire IX		§ '44
☐ PA474	Avro Lancaster I ✈	[WS-J]	'44
☐ PM631	V-S Spitfire PR.XIX ✈	[N]	'45
☐ PS915	V-S Spitfire PR.XIX✈		'45
☐ PZ865	Hawker Hurricane II ✈	(G-AMAU)	'44
☐ VP981	DH Devon C.2/2 ✈		§ '49
☐ WK518	DHC Chipmunk T.10 ✈		Can '51
☐ ZA947	Douglas Dakota III✈	[YS]	US '43

Nearby:

Boston, *12 miles.*

City of Lincoln, *20 miles.*

Cranwell Visitor Centre, *15 miles – see page 51.*

Lincolnshire Aviation Heritage Centre, *8 miles – see page 52.*

Metheringham Visitor Centre, *10 miles – see page 51.*

Navenby Heritage Room, *16 miles – see page 51.*

Thorpe Camp, *2 miles – see page 57.*

Wellingore Heritage Room, *16 miles – see page 51.*

Aircraft of the BBMF regularly change their squadron codes, Lancaster PA474 in the colours of 101 Squadron, 1985. Mike Ingham

BOMBER COUNTY AVIATION MUSEUM

Hemswell Cliff, Lincolnshire

Address: Wayne Drurey, Curator, 75 Sixhills Street, Grimsby, South Humberside, DN32 9HS

Where: Within the former RAF Hemswell (now Hemswell Cliff) north of the A631 Gainsborough to Market Rasen road. Signed from the A631 as Hemswell Antique and Craft Centre.

Open: Sundays and Bank Holidays 11am to 6pm and at other times by prior arrangement.

By rail: Gainsborough 10 miles.

Tourist: Lincoln 01522 529828.

Admission: Free, donations welcomed.

Facilities: Shop/Disabled*/Changes/Brochure.

Within the main site of the former RAF Hemswell, the museum is run by the Hemswell Aviation Society. There is a small internal display and shop and a static aircraft park. Car park and cafe facilities in the antique and craft centre close by.

Aircraft exhibits:

☐	G-AEJZ	Mignet HM.14 Flying Flea (BAPC.120)	§ Fr '36
☐	WJ975	EE Canberra T.19 [S]	'53
☐	XD445	DH Vampire T.11 [51]	'54
☐	XG195	Hawker Hunter FGA.9	'56
☐	XG506	Bristol Sycamore HR.14	'55
☐	101	Dassault Mystère IVA [8-MN]	Fr '55

Nearby:

City of Lincoln, *12 miles.*

Metheringham Visitor Centre, *18 miles – see page 51.*

National Mining Museum, Bothamsall, *18 miles.*

Navenby Heritage Room, *20 miles – see page 51.*

Skellingthorpe Heritage Room, *14 miles – see page 51.*

Wellingore Heritage Room, *20 miles – see page 51.*

Entrance hall to the Bomber County Aviation Museum.
Mike Ingham

'CARPETBAGGER' AND NORTHANTS AVIATION MUSEUMS

Harrington, Northamptonshire

Address: Sunny Vale Farm Nursery, off Lamport Road, Harrington, Northampton, NN6 9PF.
Telephone: 01604 686608.
Where: On minor road south out of Harrington village, towards Lamport, and turn right after the A14 underpass - follow signs.
Open: Easter to October at weekends and Bank Holidays, 10am to 5pm. Other times by prior appointment.
By rail: Market Harborough 5 miles.
Tourist: Market Harborough 01858 468106, Fax 01858 463168.
Admission: Adult £2, Child £1 - covers both museums.
Facilities: Toilets/Parking/Cafe*/Shop/Disabled/All/Changes/Brochure.

Opened in March 1994, this museum is centred upon the 'bomb-proof' adminstration building of what was once USAAF Station 179, home of the clandestine 492nd and 801st BGs. Within the sub-terranean building can be found a wide array of items devoted to the history of the station and to Northamptonshire at war. The latter subject is also part of the fascinating display of artefacts held in the adjacent former Paymaster's building, now the home of the Northamptonshire Aviation Society who have opened the Northants Aviation Museum. This benefits from the NAS's extensive 'dig' activity in the county.

Nearby:
City of Leicester, *18 miles*.
Foxton Locks and Inclined Plane, *8 miles*.
Lamport Hall and Brampton Railway Museum, *4 miles*.
Naseby Battlefield and Farm Museum, *6 miles*.
City of Northampton, *12 miles*.
Percy Pilcher Museum, *12 miles – see page 55*.
Rutland Water, *20 miles*.

Inside the 'bomb-proof' Carpetbagger museum. Ken Ellis

DERBY INDUSTRIAL MUSEUM

Derby, Derbyshire

Address: Silk Mill Lane, off Full Street, Derby, DE1 3AR.
Telephone: 01332 255308, Fax 01332 255804.
Where: South of the inner ring road (the A52), close to the cathedral and well signed.
Open: Monday 11am to 5pm, Tuesday to Saturday 10am to 5pm. Sundays and Bank Holidays 2pm to 5pm.
By bus: Derby's main bus station is a short walk away. By rail: Derby, walking distance.
Tourist: Derby 01332 255802.
Admission: Free.
Facilities: Toilets/Parking/Shop/Disabled/All/ Changes/Brochure.

Recently redeveloped, the aero engine gallery – effectively a shrine to local producer Rolls-Royce – is an absorbing and beautifully presented look at development from the Eagle to the mighty RB.211. The museum building, the Silk Mill, was one of the world's first modern factories, originally built in 1702. Other exhibits concentrate on textiles, the iron industry, railways, a working beam engine and many other aspects of Derby's industrial heritage.

Nearby:

Brewery Museum, Burton-on-Trent, *12 miles*.
City of Nottingham, *12 miles*.
City of Derby city centre, cathedral and museum all close to. River Trent runs past the museum.
Heights of Abraham, Matlock, *16 miles*.
Snibston Discovery Park, *14 miles – see page 56*.
Tramway Museum, Crich, *12 miles*.

Part of the extensive aero engine gallery at Derby. Ken Ellis

LINCOLNSHIRE AVIATION HERITAGE TRAIL

North Kesteven District Council has developed an award-winning Airfield Heritage Trail around the airfield sites within its boundaries. Most of the sites have been marked with designator signs and information boards. Linking all this together is a well produced booklet describing each site and available from the Sleaford Tourist Information Centre. Additional to this North Kesteven has developed two other centres, one at Cranwell and one at Metheringham which can be visited independently of the trail or used as central points when on it. (West Lindsey District Council has produced a detailed booklet on the airfields within its 'beat' and early in 1995 followed this up with a further set of leaflets on the district's memorials and airfields.) There are also three heritage rooms within the council which have sections dealing with the local airfield. Add to this the museums of the county and there is much to do here!

CRANWELL AVIATION HERITAGE CENTRE

Address: c/o Tourist Information Centre, The Mill, Moneys Yard, Carre Street, Sleaford, Lincs, NG34 7TW.
Telephone: 01529 488490.
Where: Signposted just off the A17 (to the south of RAF Cranwell) on the minor road to North and South Rauceby.
Open: Open 9am to 5pm daily (closes 4pm in winter months) other than Xmas and New Year.
By rail: Sleaford 3 miles.
Tourist: The centre is itself a TIC (see number above), or Sleaford 01529 414249.
Admission: Free.
Facilities: Toilets/Parking/Shop/Disabled/All/ Brochure.

Located close to the RAF base, the centre charts the history of Cranwell and gives notes on the other airfields on the Lincolnshire Airfield Trail. Tourist Information Centre adjacent.

METHERINGHAM VISITOR CENTRE

Address: c/o Tourist Information Centre, The Mill, Moneys Yard, Carre Street, Sleaford, Lincs, NG34 7TW.
Telephone: 01526 378270.
Where: At Westmoor Farm, Martin Moor, Metheringham. Signposted off the B1189.
Open: 10am to 5pm April to November, or at other times by appointment.
By rail: Metheringham 1 mile.
Tourist: Sleaford 01529 414249.
Admission: Free.
Facilities: Toilets/Parking/Shop/Disabled/All/ Brochure.

Outside the centre is a memorial garden and an impressive memorial to 106 Squadron. Inside are many displays including rolls of honour and much on the history of the bomber base. (See overleaf.)

Additionally, there are three Heritage Rooms:

NAVENBY HERITAGE ROOM: Next to the Post Office in Navenby on the A607 south of Lincoln. Open all year 9am to 5.30pm Mon/Tue/Thu/Fri and 9.am to 12.30pm Wednesday and Sunday. Exhibits on local history including the RAF in the area.

SKELLINGTHORPE HERITAGE ROOM: Near the Community Centre at Skellingthorpe, north of the A46, west of Lincoln. Open 10am to 5pm daily April to October and 10am to 4pm November to March. Located in what was the weighbridge office of the former railway station with displays on the former airfield, 50 and 61 Squadrons and F/O Manser VC.

WELLINGORE HERITAGE ROOM: On the A607 in the village, south of Lincoln. Open daily 9am to 5pm. Displays include local airfields, including RAF Wellingore, and local history.

Above: **Lincolnshire Airfield Heritage Trail marker at Metheringham.** Ken Ellis

LINCOLNSHIRE AVIATION HERITAGE CENTRE

Address: East Kirkby, near Spilsby, Lincs, PE23 4DE.
Telephone: 01790 763207.
Where: On the A155 west of Spilsby, signposted.
Open: Open Easter to October Monday to Saturday 10am to 5pm, last admission 4pm, and November to Easter Monday to Saturday 10am to 4pm, last admission 3pm.
Note – not open on Sundays.
By rail: Boston 12 miles.
Tourist: Woodhall Spa* 01507 600206.
Boston 01205 356656.
Admission: Adult £3, OAP £2.50, Child £1.50.
Facilities: Toilets/Parking/Cafe/Shop/Disabled/Kids/All/Changes/Brochure.

Using part of the former bomber airfield of East Kirkby, the museum has grown around the well restored and fitted out watch tower. Main centre of attraction is undoubtedly the Lancaster, which does ground runs occasionally. There are wide-ranging displays dedicated to the men and machines who flew from East Kirkby and from Lincolnshire in general. Other exhibitions include the RAF Escaping Society, military vehicles, an air raid shelter and items excavated by the Lincolnshire Aircraft Recovery Group.

Aircraft exhibits:

☐	AE436	HP Hampden I fuselage	§ '41
☐	BL655	Supermarine Spitfire V wreck	'42
☐	NP294	Percival Proctor IV [TB-M]	'44
☐	NX611	Avro Lancaster VII (G-ASXX)	
☐		[DX-C/LE-C]	'45
☐	VP293	Avro Shackleton T.4 nose [A]	'51
☐	WH957	EE Canberra E.15 nose	'55
☐	WW421	Percival Provost T.1 [P-B]	'54
☐	–	CASA 2-111D (He 111H) nose	§ c54
☐	–	Colditz Cock glider replica (BAPC.90)	'44
☐	–	Druine Turbulent (BAPC.154)	§ Fr c70

Nearby:

Battle of Britain Memorial Flight Visitor Centre, *8 miles – see page 47.*
Metheringham Visitor Centre, *16 miles – see page 51.*
Thorpe Camp, *10 miles – see page 57.*

Below: **The famous watch tower at East Kirkby.** Ken Ellis

NEWARK AIR MUSEUM
Newark, Nottinghamshire

Address: The Airfield, Winthorpe, Newark, Notts, NG24 2NY

Telephone: 01636 707170

Where: North east of Newark, off the A46 Lincoln Road, on Newark Showground. Signposted from the A1

Open: Daily, excluding December 24-26. April-October weekdays 10am to 5pm, weekends 10am to 6pm; November-March every day 10am to 4pm

Admission: Adult £3.25, child/concessions £2.00

By bus: Pathfinder bus to Collingham will drop near museum.

By rail: Newark Northgate 3 miles

Tourist: Newark 01636 78962, Fax 01636 612274

Facilities: Toilets/Parking/Cafe/Shop/Disabled/All/Changes/Brochure

Located on part of the former RAF Winthorpe airfield, Newark Air Museum is a long established collection centred essentially on post-war RAF aircraft, including a 'speciality' of Gloster Meteor variants. Large aircraft display hall with subsidiary displays including the history of RAF Winthorpe, Royal Observer Corps, ejector seats and a Flying Flea 'workshop'. Restoration workshop on site – visitors can peak at progress. Engine display hall with extensive collection of piston and jet engines, large exhibition hall with artefacts from all eras. Phantom and Gnat cockpit simulators plus Jet Provost nose section available to children to sit in at times. Avro Shackleton maritime patroller, Avro Vulcan V-bomber and Handley Page Hastings crew trainer occasionally open to the public, at extra charge. Major improvements to the entrance hall, shop etc underway. Special events organised – details from the museum.

Aircraft exhibits:

☐ G-AHRI	DH Dove 1		'48
☐ 'G-MAZY'	DH Tiger Moth		c40
☐ G-ANXB	DH Heron 1		'55
☐ G-MBUE	MBA Tiger Cub 440 microlight		'82
☐ VH-UTH	General Aircraft Monospar ST-12	§	'35
☐ KF532	North American Harvard IIB cockpit	US	'45
☐ TG517	Handley Page Hastings T.5		'48
☐ VL348	Avro Anson C.19	§	'46
☐ VR249	Percival Prentice T.1 [FA-EL]		'48
☐ VZ608	Gloster Meteor FR.9 engine test-bed		'50
☐ VZ634	Gloster Meteor T.7		'49
☐ WF369	Vickers Varsity T.1 [F]		'51
☐ WH863	EE Canberra T.17 cockpit		'53
☐ WH904	EE Canberra T.19 [04]		'54
☐ WK277	Supermarine Swift FR.5 [N]		'55
☐ WM913	Hawker Sea Hawk FB.3 [456-J]		'54
☐ WR977	Avro Shackleton MR.3/3 [B]		'57
☐ WS692	Gloster Meteor NF.14		'53
☐ WT651	Hawker Hunter F.1 [C]		'54
☐ WT933	Bristol Sycamore 3		'52
☐ WV606	Percival Provost T.1 [P-B]		'55
☐ WV787	EE Canberra B.2/8		'52
☐ WW217	DH Sea Venom FAW.21 [736]		'55
☐ WX905	DH Venom NF.3		'54
☐ XD515	DH Vampire T.11		'54
☐ XD593	DH Vampire T.11 [50]		'54
☐ XE317	Bristol Sycamore HR.14		'56
☐ XH992	Gloster Javelin FAW.8		'58
☐ XJ560	DH Sea Vixen FAW.2 [242]		'57
☐ XL149	Blackburn Beverley C.1 cockpit		'57
☐ XL764	Saunders Roe Skeeter AOP.12		'58
☐ XM383	Hunting Jet Provost T.3A [90]		'59
☐ XM594	Avro Vulcan B.2		'63
☐ XM685	Westland Whirlwind HAS.7 [513-PO]	US	'58
☐ XN573	Hunting Jet Provost T.3 nose		'61
☐ XN819	Armstrong Whitworth Argosy C.1 cockpit		'61
☐ XN964	Blackburn Buccaneer S.1 [613-LM]		'63
☐ XP226	Fairey Gannet AEW.3 [073-E]		'62
☐ XS417	English Electric Lightning T.5		'64
☐ XT200	Bell Sioux AH.1 (Westland)	US	'66
☐ AR-107	SAAB S.35XD Draken	Sw	'68

☐ 83	Dassault Mystère IVA [8-MS]	Fr '56
☐ '5547'	Lockheed T-33A 'T-Bird' (19036)	US '51
☐ 42223	NA F-100D Super Sabre	US '54
☐ 56321	SAAB Safir (G-BKPY)	Swn '56
☐ –	Lee Richards Annular Biplane replica (BAPC.20)	§ '11
☐ –	Mignet HM.14 Flying Flea (BAPC.43)	Fr '36
☐ –	Mignet HM.14 Flying Flea fuselage (BAPC.101)	Fr '36
☐ –	Zurowski ZP.1 homebuilt helicopter (BAPC.183)	c75

Also:

Activities of Newark Gliding Club, when weather permits, can be seen to advantage from the museum car park. Newark Showground is host to a wide range of special events during the year, including the quarterly international antique and collectors fair which is a huge event. During such shows and events a visit to both the showground and the museum is easily achieved.

Nearby:

Belvoir Castle, *14 miles*.
City of Lincoln, *13 miles*.
City of Nottingham, *18 miles*.
Museum of Dolls and Bygone Childhood, Cromwell, *4 miles*.
National Mining Museum, Bothamsall, *14 miles*.
Papplewick Pumping Station and Miniature Railway, *14 miles*.
Cranwell Heritage Centre, *13 miles – see page 51.*
Metheringham Visitor Centre, *16 miles – see page 51.*
Sherwood Forest and Visitor Centre, *14 miles.*

Inside Newark's aircraft exhibition hall, Venom and Anson foremost. Newark Air Museum

PERCY PILCHER MUSEUM

Stanford Hall, Leicestershire

Address: Stanford Hall, Lutterworth, Leicestershire, LE17 6DH.
Telephone: 01788 860250, Fax 01788 860870.
Where: Signposted off an unclassified road north east of Swinford, close to junction 19 of the M1 (M6/A14/M1 interchange).
Open: Saturdays and Sundays, Easter to September 2.30pm to 5.30pm, also Bank Holidays and the Tuesdays following, same times.
By rail: Rugby 7 miles.
Tourist: Rugby 01788 535348, Fax 01788 573289.
Admission: House and grounds, Adult £3.20, Child £1.50.
Facilities: Toilets/Parking/Cafe/Shop/Disabled/All/Brochure/X

Within the hall is a small display devoted to the life and times of Sir Percy Pilcher, including a fine replica of the Hawk glider. Aviation pioneer Pilcher was killed in the grounds of the hall whilst flying the Hawk in September 1899. Also at the hall is an outstanding collection of motorcycles, viewable at extra charge. The 17th century hall is magnificent, the gardens equally so, boasting the River Avon running through them. Regular special events staged in the grounds during the season, including occasional balloon rallies.

Aircraft exhibit:

☐ –	Pilcher Hawk replica (BAPC.45)		1896

Nearby:
Bosworth Battlefield and Light Railway, *20 miles.*
Carpetbagger Aviation Museum, *12 miles –* see page 49.
City of Coventry, *16 miles.*
City of Leicester, *20 miles.*
Midland Air Museum, *16 miles – see page 29.*
City of Northampton, *16 miles.*

The Hawk in flight at Eynsford, Kent, 1896. Pioneer Sir Percy Pilcher was killed in this machine at Stanford Hall in 1899. Kent Libraries

SNIBSTON DISCOVERY PARK

Coalville, Leicestershire

Address: Ashby Road, Coalville, Leicestershire, LE6 2LN.

Telephone: 01530 510851, Fax 01530 813301, 24 hour information line 01530 813256.

Where: Well signed off the A50 Coalville road.

Open: Daily 10am to 6pm, April to October, 10am to 5pm November to March, except December 25-26.

By bus: Midland Fox bus services.

By rail: Loughborough 6 miles.

Tourist: On site, 01530 813608, Fax 01530 813301.

Admission: Adult £4, Child/cons £2.75, Family ticket £10.

Facilities: Toilets/Parking/Cafe/Shop/Disabled/Kids/All/Brochure.

Tracing the history of Leicestershire's industrial heritage in a vivid manner are five galleries: textiles and fashion; engineering; extractive industries; science and transport. In the latter can be found an

Auster AOP.9 marking the aircraft production undertaken in the county. Outside is the 100 acre discovery park which includes a colliery tour. Many special events and exhibitions staged during the year.

Aircraft exhibits:

☐ G-AIJK	Auster J/4	§ '46
☐ G-AJRH	Auster J/1N Alpha	§ '47
☐ VZ728	Reid & Sigrist Desford Trainer (G-AGOS)	§ '45
☐ XP280	Auster AOP.9	'61

Nearby:

Aeropark and Visitor Centre, *8 miles – see page 46.*

Bosworth Battlefield and Light Railway, *8 miles.*

City of Derby, *14 miles.*

Derby Industrial Museum, *14 miles – see page 50.*

Donington Motor Racing Museum, *8 miles.*

City of Leicester, *10 miles.*

City of Nottingham, *16 miles.*

Auster AOP.9 XP280 on display at Snibston, was built at nearby Rearsby, in 1961. Ken Ellis

THORPE CAMP VISITOR CENTRE

Tattershall Thorpe, Lincolnshire

Address: Thorpe Camp Preservation Group, 14 Thorpe Road, Tattershall, Lincolnshire, LN4 4NX.
Where: On the B1192 south of Woodhall Spa.
Open: Open Sunday afternoons and Bank Holidays 2pm to 5pm, Easter to October.
By rail: Lincoln 18 miles.
Tourist: Woodhall Spa* 01526 353775, Fax 01507 600206. Lincoln 01522 529828.
Admission: By donation.
Facilities: Toilets/Parking/Cafe*/Shop/Disabled*/All/Changes/Brochure.

Located on the former No 1 Communal Site of RAF Woodhall Spa airfield – once base to 617 and 627 Squadrons – this newly established museum serves to chart the history of the airfield and the units that served on it. Other displays include life in wartime Lincolnshire, all supported by a large amount of artefacts and photographs.

Aircraft exhibit:

☐ G-AJOZ   Fairchild Argus II   § US '42

Nearby:
Boston, *12 miles.*
City of Lincoln, *20 miles.*
Cranwell Visitor Centre, *15 miles – see page 51.*
Lincolnshire Aviation Heritage Centre, *8 miles – see page 52.*
Metheringham Visitor Centre, *10 miles – see page 51.*
Navenby Heritage Room, *16 miles – see page 51.*
Wellingore Heritage Room, *16 miles – see page 51.*

Some of the buildings that comprise Thorpe Camp, once part of the domestic site of RAF Woodhall Spa. Within can be found an expanding collection devoted to the history of the airfield and life in wartime Lincolnshire. Ken Ellis

ALSO IN
THE EAST MIDLANDS

**BRUNTINGTHORPE, BRITISH AVIATION HER-
ITAGE AND THE LIGHTNING PRESERVATION
GROUP** operate from this Leicestershire airfield.
The former have become famous as the owners of
Avro Vulcan B.2 XH558 along with HP Victor K.2
XM715 plus a growing collection of other post-war
hardware and Boeing 747-100 F-BPVE which flew
in during September 1994. Plans to open regularly
are not yet finalised but the annual 'Big Thunder'
airshow allows close access. Visits by prior
arrangement only, send SAE to C Walton (Aviation
Division) Ltd, Bruntingthorpe Airfield, Bruntingthorpe, Lutterworth, Leics, LE17 5QH. The Lightning
Preservation Group keep in fast taxiable condition
two EE Lightning F.6s, XR728 and XS904. Regular
'running' days are staged and these are advertised
in the aviation press. Send SAE for details to LPG,
95, Thornhill, North Weald, Essex, CM16 6DP.

BINBROOK, LIGHTNING ASSOCIATION are
based on the former RAF airfield and they maintain
F.6 XR724 in near airworthy condition. They stage
an annual 'Lightning Rally' at the airfield to unite all
Lightning lovers and publish an excellent house
journal. SAE for details to Lightning Association,
Binbrook Airfield, Lincolnshire, LN3 6HF.

ROLLS-ROYCE HERITAGE TRUST, Coventry
Branch. While the branch would seem better suit-
ed to the Heart of England, the closure of the Rolls-
Royce factory at Parkside in Coventry in 1994
meant that the excellent collection of aero
engines, cars and much else restored and kept by
the branch had to relocate to Mickleover, Derbyshire, to premises within the Rolls-Royce Training Centre. There is an annual open day but visits
are welcomed at other times by prior arrangement.
Send SAE to W Westacott, Rolls-Royce Aerospace
Training Centre, Station Road, Mickleover, Derby.

Rolls-Royce Heritage Trust Coventry Branch is custodian to a large aero engine collection. Ken Ellis

NORTHUMBRIA AND CUMBRIA
Cleveland, Cumbria, Durham, Northumberland and Tyne & Wear

Scotland

NEWCASTLE

CARLISLE

Yorkshire & Humberside

1 Solway Aviation Society
2 North East Aircraft Museum
3 Steamboat Museum
4 RAF Millom Museum

North West

Cumbria Tourist Board
Ashleigh, Holly Road, Windermere, Cumbria, LA23 2AQ
Tel: 015394 44444 Fax: 015394 44041

Northumbria Tourist Board
Aykley Heads, Durham, County Durham, DH2 5UX
Tel: 0191 384 0899 Fax: 0191 386 0899

NORTH EAST AIRCRAFT MUSEUM
Sunderland, Tyne & Wear

Address: Old Washington Road, Sunderland, Tyne & Wear, SR5 3HZ.
Telephone: 0191 5190662.
Where: North of the A123, off the A1290 Washington Road, follow signs for the Nissan plant.
Open: Open every day 10am to 5pm (or dusk in winter).
By rail: Sunderland 3 miles.
Tourist: Sunderland 0191 5650960 or '5650990, Fax 0191 5653352.
Admission: TBA.
Facilities: Toilets/Parking/Cafe*/Shop/Disabled*/All/Changes/X.

A large and impressive collection of aircraft, with two display halls and a workshop. The large entrance foyer and 'small artefact' hall is undergoing a refurbishment to further improve the facilities available to visitors. Themes include NATO combat aircraft, the Royal Observer Corps and search and rescue. The story of aviation in the north east of England is also given good treatment. The museum has a vigorous restoration programme and visitors can keep an eye on the progress of airframes in the workshop.

Aircraft exhibits:

☐ 'G-ADVU'*	Mignet HM.14 Flying Flea (BAPC.211)	Fr '36
☐ G-APTW	Westland Widgeon 2	'59
☐ G-ARHX	DH Dove 8	'61
☐ G-AWRS	Avro Anson C.19	§ '46
☐ G-BEEX	DH Comet 4C nose	'61
☐ G-MBDL	AES Lone Ranger microlight	§ '81
☐ G-OGIL	Short SD.330-100	'81
☐ 'G-BAGJ'	Westland Gazelle 1 (G-SFTA))	§ Fr '72
☐ RH746	Bristol Brigand TF.1	§ '46
☐ VV217	DH Vampire FB.5	§ '48
☐ VX577	Vickers Valetta C.2	'50
☐ WA577	Bristol Sycamore 3	'49
☐ WB685	DHC Chipmunk T.10 fuselage	Can '50
☐ WD790	Gloster Meteor NF.11 nose	'52
☐ WD889	Fairey Firefly AS.5 cockpit	'53
☐ WG724	Westland Dragonfly HR.5	US '52
☐ WJ639	EE Canberra TT.18	'54
☐ WK198	Supermarine Swift F.4 fuselage	§ '53
☐ WL181	Gloster Meteor F.8 [X]	'54
☐ WN516	BP Balliol T.2 cockpit	§ '54
☐ WZ518	DH Vampire T.11	'53
☐ WZ767	Slingsby Grasshopper TX.1	'55
☐ XG518	Bristol Sycamore HR.14	'55
☐ XG523	Bristol Sycamore HR.14 cockpit	'55
☐ XG680	DH Sea Venom FAW.22 [438]	'57
☐ XL319	Avro Vulcan B.2	'61
☐ XM660	Westland Whirlwind HAS.7	US '58
☐ XN258	Westland Whirlwind HAR.9 [589-CU]	US '59
☐ XP627	Hunting Jet Provost T.4	'62
☐ XT236	Westland Sioux AH.1	§ US '66
☐ XW276	Westland Gazelle 03	Fr '70
☐ ZF594	EE Lightning F.53	'68
☐ A-522	FMA Pucara	Arg c76
☐ E-419	Hawker Hunter F.51	'56
☐ 146	Dassault Mystère IVA	Fr '55
☐ 6171	NA F-86D-35-NA Sabre	US '51
☐ 26541	Republic F-84F Thunderstreak	US '52
☐ 42157	NA F-100D Super Sabre [11-ML]	US '54
☐ 54439	Lockheed T-33A T-Bird [WI]	US '54
☐ –	Bensen B.7 gyroglider (BAPC.119)	US c67
☐ –	Brown Helicopter (BAPC.96)	§ '62
☐ –	Chargus Olympus hang glider (BAPC.228)	§ c81
☐ –	HP C-10A Jetstream cockpit (mock-up)	'69
☐ –	Luton LA-4 Minor (BAPC.97)	§ '37

Nearby:
Beamish North of England Open Air Museum, *10 miles.*
Maritime Museum, Hartlepool, *20 miles.*
City of Newcastle upon Tyne, *8 miles.*
Ryhope Engines Museum, *7 miles.*
City of Sunderland, *3 miles.*

RAF MILLOM MUSEUM
Haverigg, Cumbria

Address: South Copeland Aviation Group, c/o John Nixon, RAF Millom Museum Project, HM Prison Haverigg, Millom, Cumbria, LA18 4NA.

Where: On the Bankhead Estate, North Lane, Haverigg, adjacent to HMP Haverigg.

Open: Open every Sunday afternoon from 12.30pm to 5.30pm Easter to end of November. Other times by prior arrangement.

By bus: Services from Millom.

By rail: Millom 2 miles.

Tourist: Barrow-in-Furness 01229 870156, Fax 01229 432289.

Admission: Free, donations welcome.

Facilities: Toilets/Parking/Kids/All/Changes.

A small museum housed in buildings that were previously part of the former RAF Millom airfield –
now largely occupied by HMP Haverigg. The Flying Flea was completed in Early April 1995 and it is planned to put it on show when the second display building opens in late 1995. Displays chart the history of the airfield and of military aviation in the region, including the many crashes in local waters and on the surrounding hills.

Aircraft exhibits:

☐ 'G-ADRX'	Mignet HM.14 Flying Flea (BAPC.231)	§ Fr c36
☐ XD425	Vampire T.11 nose [16]	§ '54

Nearby:

The Lake District, *18 miles*.

Ravenglass and Eskdale Miniature Railway, *16 miles*.

Sellafield Visitor Centre, *18 miles*.

Steamboat Museum, *18 miles – see page 63*.

Below: **A view of the main display hall at the North East Aircraft Museum.** Ken Ellis

Below: **Inside the RAF Millom Museum, devoted to the history of the airfield and the local area.** Ken Ellis

SOLWAY
AVIATION SOCIETY
Carlisle Airport, Cumbria

Address: Solway Aviation Society Ltd, c/o
Carlisle Airport, Crosby-on-Eden, Carlisle,
Cumbria, CA6 4NW.

Where: Carlisle Airport, on the B6264 east of
Carlisle and signposted.

Open: Sundays 2pm to 4pm. Other times by prior
arrangement.

By rail: Carlisle, 6 miles.

Tourist: Carlisle 01228 512444, Fax 01228
511758.

Admission: TBA.

Facilities: Parking/Shop/Changes/X.

The Solway Aviation Society maintains a small visitor centre and collection of aircraft at the airport. On occasions the Vulcan is open to inspection and the systems are run up. Within the visitor centre are displays relating to the airfields of Cumbria and the Spadeadam rocket range.

Aircraft exhibits:

☐ WE188	EE Canberra T.4	'52
☐ WS832	Gloster Meteor NF.14	'54
☐ WV198	Westland Whirlwind HAR.21	
	(G-BJWY)	US '52
☐ WZ515	DH Vampire T.11	'53
☐ XJ823	Avro Vulcan B.2	'61
☐ ZF583	EE Lightning F.53	'68

Nearby:
City of Carlisle, *6 miles.*
Hadrian's Hall and Roman Forts, *12 and 20 miles.*

Vulcan and Lightning nose to tail at Carlisle. It is possible to go inside the Vulcan where great effort has been made to make the cockpit 'live', including taped radio message chatter. Ken Ellis

STEAMBOAT MUSEUM

Windermere, Cumbria

Address: Rayrigg Road, Windermere, Cumbria, LA23 1BN.

Telephone: 01539 445565.

Where: Signposted within the town, on the lakefront.

Open: Open Easter to October, daily 10am to 5pm.

By bus: Several bus services into Windermere.

By rail: Windermere, 1 mile.

Tourist: Windermere 01539 446499, Fax 01539 447439.

Admission: TBA.

Facilities: Toilets/Parking/Shop/Disabled*/All/Changes.

Within the collection of unique Victorian and Edwardian steam launches, many of which still cruise the lake can be found the equally unique waterglider, which was converted in 1943 to flying-boat guise for trials. Along with the waterglider is a display showing aviation on and around the lake since 1911.

Aircraft exhibit:

☐ BGA.266 Slingsby T.1 Falcon waterglider '36

Nearby:

The Lake District and its many attractions – Ambleside, *6 miles;* Lakeside to Haverthwaite Railway, *6 miles;* Coniston, *8 miles.*

Kendal, *8 miles.*

Keswick, *20 miles.*

RAF Millom Museum, *18 miles – see page 61.*

A conversion of a standard Slingsby Falcon, the waterglider was the brainchild of T C Pattinson and it first flew in 1943. It was hoped that it would lead to water-launching troop-carrying gliders for use in the liberation of Europe. Ken Ellis

1745 and 1780

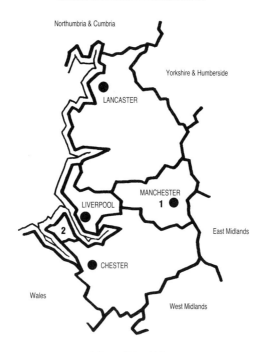

NORTH WEST ENGLAND
Cheshire, Greater Manchester, Lancashire, Merseyside

Northumbria & Cumbria

Yorkshire & Humberside

LANCASTER

MANCHESTER
1

LIVERPOOL

2

East Midlands

CHESTER

Wales

West Midlands

1 Museum of Science & Industry
  Manchester
2 Warship Preservation Trust

North West Tourist Board
Swan House, Swan Meadow Road, Wigan Pier, Wigan, WN3 5BB
Tel: 01942 821222 Fax: 01942 820002

MUSEUM OF SCIENCE AND INDUSTRY AIR & SPACE GALLERY

Manchester, Greater Manchester

Address: Liverpool Road, Manchester, M3 4JP.
Telephone: 0161 832 2244
or 24-hour information line 0161 832 1830,
Fax 0161 833 2184.
Where: Close to the end of the A57 in central Manchester, well signposted.
Open: Every day from 10am to 5pm, including Bank Holidays but excluding December 23-25.
By bus: Metrolink tram stop nearby. No 33 from Piccadilly Gardens stops outside.
By rail: Deansgate, walking distance.
Tourist: Manchester 0161 2343157 or '2343158, Fax 0161 2369900.
Admission: Adult £4, Child/cons £2.
Facilities: Toilets/Parking/Cafe/Shop/Disabled/All/Changes/Brochure.

The air and space gallery of the Museum of Science and Industry is just the tip of the iceberg in this amazing seven acre site. The aviation hall includes a gallery that offers interesting aspects and angles on the airframes. The Trident cockpit offers a close view of the world inside an airliner and the Super-X simulator can take all comers for the nearest thing to a real flight. The space gallery includes interactive displays. The remainder of the museum has to be seen as well, including the power hall with working steam and other engines, the world's oldest station (Liverpool Street) complete with a variety of rolling stock and locomotives, underground Manchester – take a walk through a sewer – and much more.

Aircraft exhibits:

☐ G-EBZM	Avro Avian IIIA		'28
☐ G-ABAA	Avro 504K		
☐ G-ADAH	DH Dragon Rapide	§	'35
☐ G-APUD	Bensen B.7M	US	'59
☐ G-AWZP	HS Trident 3B-101 nose		'72
☐ G-AYTA	MS Rallye Club	§	'71
☐ 'T9707'	Miles Magister I (G-AKKR)		'40
☐ MT847	Supermarine Spitfire XIV [AX-H]		'45
☐ WB440	Fairey Firefly AS.6 cockpit		'47
☐ WG763	EE P.1A		'55
☐ WP270	Slingsby Eton TX.1		'55
☐ WR960	Avro Shackleton AEW.2		'54
☐ WT619	Hawker Hunter F.1		'54
☐ WZ736	Avro 707A		'53
☐ XG454	Bristol Belvedere HC.1		'62
☐ XL824	Bristol Sycamore HR.14		'57
☐ J-1172	DH Vampire FB.6		c53
☐ 997	Yokosuka MXY-7 Ohka 11 suicide weapon		Ja '45
☐ –	Cayley Glider replica (BAPC.89)		1853
☐ –	Roe Triplane replica (BAPC.6)		'09
☐ –	Volmer VJ-23 Swingwing microlight (BAPC.175)		US '78
☐ –	Wood Ornithopter (BAPC.182)	§	c65

Nearby:

East Lancashire Railway, *10 miles.*
Granada Studios Experience, *adjacent.*
Manchester Airport Viewing Park, *8 miles.*
Manchester City Centre walking distance.
Manchester Tramway Museum, *2 miles.*
Quarry Bank Mill, *10 miles.*

See overleaf.

Relaxed scene around the museum's Avro 504K during its joy-riding heyday, mid-1930s.
Museum of Science & Industry

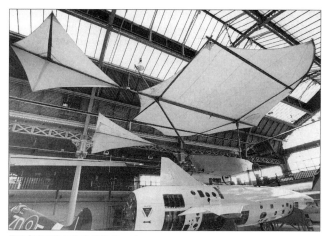

Above: **Cayley glider replica inside the impressive building at Manchester. Despite its improbable looks, the replica flew well.**

Below: **General view of Manchester's Air and Space Gallery, Avro 707 in the foreground.** Both Alan Curry

Above: **Manchester's Belvedere under test at Filton, near Bristol, prior to acceptance by the RAF in July 1960. The large 'end-plates' to the tailplane were added later.** Westland

WARSHIP PRESERVATION TRUST

Birkenhead Docks, Merseyside

Address: Warship Preservation Trust, Birkenhead, L41 1DJ.
Telephone: 0151 650 1573, plus Fax.
Where: Birkenhead Docks, signposted.
Open: Open daily from 10am to 5pm.
By bus: Several services pass close by.
By rail: Birkenhead, 1 mile.
Tourist: Birkenhead 0151 6476780.
Admission: TBA.
Facilities: Toilets/Parking/Cafe/Shop/All.

HMS *Plymouth* has been berthed in Birkenhead since 1991 and has proved to be a popular attraction, including the Wasp helicopter in the hangar. Also on public view is the submarine HMS *Onyx*. During summer weekends and school holidays the Liverpool Bar Lightship is also available for inspection.

Aircraft exhibit:

☐ XS570	Westland Wasp HAS.1 [445]	'65

Nearby:
Boat Museum, *10 miles.*
City of Chester, *14 miles.*
City of Liverpool, *3 miles.*
Mersey Ferries, *1 mile.*
Mouldsworth Motor Museum, *18 miles.*

ALSO IN THE NORTH WEST

The **GRIFFIN TRUST** is working hard to establish a major transport and heritage collection within the historic hangars of the former Hooton Park airfield, now largely occupied by Vauxhall Motors. For 1995, until October there are guided tours on the last Sunday of the month. Otherwise inspection is by prior permission only. The Aeroplane Collection are busy establishing their extensive collection of light aircraft on sight, many of which are viewable during the tour. Send an SAE to Griffin Trust, Hooton Park, North Road, Ellesmere Port, South Wirral, Merseyside, L65 1BQ, or call 0151 3502598.

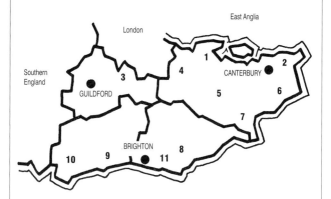

SOUTH EAST ENGLAND
Kent, Surrey, East Sussex, West Sussex

1 Royal Engineers Museum
2 Hurricane & Spitfire Memorial Building
3 Brooklands Museum
4 Shoreham Aircraft Preservation Society

5 Lashenden Air Warfare Museum
6 Kent Battle of Britain Museum
7 Brenzett Aeronautical Museum
8 Foulkes-Halbard Collection
9 Museum of D-Day Aviation

10 Tangmere Military Aviation Museum
11 Newhaven Fort

South East Tourist Board
The Old Brew House, Warwick Park, Tunbridge Wells, Kent, TN2 5TU
Tel: 01892 540766 Fax: 01892 511008

BRENZETT AERONAUTICAL MUSEUM

Brenzett, Kent

Address: Ivychurch Road, Brenzett, Romney Marsh, Kent TN29 0EE.
Telephone: 01233 627911.
Where: Brenzett in on the A259 north west of New Romney. The museum is on an unclasssified road to Ivychurch.
Open: Sundays and Bank Holidays from Easter to end of October, 11am to 5.30pm and additionally Tuesdays, Wednesdays and Thursdays, July to end of October from 2pm to 5.30pm.
By rail: Rye 7 miles.
Tourist: Rye 01797 226696.
Admission: Adult £1.75, OAP £1, Child 50p.
Facilities: Toilets/Parking/Shop/Kids/All/ Changes/Brochure.

Using buildings occupied by the Women's Land Army (WLA) during the Second World War, the museum overlooks the former Advanced Landing Ground (ALG) that carried the names of Brenzett or Ivychurch and was used briefly during the run-up to D-Day and beyond. There is a small static park of aircraft and large artefacts and an impressive memorial to those who worked and fought from all of Kent's ALGs. The museum contains a wealth of material on Brenzett, military aviation in Kent and includes a display on life in the WLA.

Aircraft exhibits:

☐ G-AGPG	Avro XIX Srs 2 (Anson)	§ '45
☐ G-AMSM	Douglas Dakota 4 nose	US '43
☐ V7350	Hawker Hurricane I wreck	'40
☐ WH657	EE Canberra B.2	'52
☐ XK625	DH Vampire T.11 nose [12]	'56
☐ –	EE Canberra PR.7 nose	§ c53

Nearby:

Folkestone and Hastings, *16 miles.*
Kent and East Sussex Railway, *9 miles.*
Kent Battle of Britain Museum, *16 miles.*
Lashenden Air Warfare Museum, *14 miles – see page 75.*
Romney, Hythe & Dymchurch Railway, *12 miles.*

Below: **One of the display halls at Brenzett.** Ken Ellis

BROOKLANDS MUSEUM
Weybridge, Surrey

Address: The Clubhouse, Brooklands Road,
Weybridge, Surrey, KT13 0QN.
Telephone: 01932 857381, Fax 01932 855465.
Where: On the B374 south of Weybridge, access
from Junctions 10 or 12 of the M25.
Open: Tuesday to Sunday 10am to 5pm (last
entry 4pm), Easter to October. Winter months,
10am to 4pm, last entry is 3pm. Note: closed
on Mondays. Normally closed Good Friday,
Xmas and New Year. Pre-arranged guided
tours available Tuesdays to Fridays, by
telephoning the museum.
By bus: Local services out of Weybridge.
By rail: Weybridge 2 miles.
Tourist: Twickenham 0181 8911411.
Admission: Adult £4.50, Cons/Child £2.50,
Family ticket £12.50.
Facilities: Toilets/Parking/Cafe/Shop/Disabled/
All/Changes/Brochure.

Brooklands has always been a heady combination
of aviation and motor racing and so it remains. On
the aeronautical side there is Barnes Wallis' design
office, the stratospheric test chamber and the balloon hangar, the world's first flight ticket office, the
reconstruction of A V Roe's 1908 aircraft shed and
the finishing straight hangar which houses, amongst
others, the famed Loch Ness Wellington 'R-
Robert'. On the motor racing side there is the clubhouse, Malcolm Campbell's workshop, the car
collection, the hill climb, and the banked circuit.
There are many special events, both wheel and
wing-borne and a variety of exhibitions staged
each year.

Aircraft exhibits:

☐ A40-AB	BAC VC-10 1103		'64
☐ 'D-12-354'	Aachen Rheinland ✈ (CPZ)	Gr c33	
☐ F-BGEQ	DH Tiger Moth	§ '43	
☐ 'G-EBED'	Vickers Viking replica		'19
☐ 'G-AACA'	Avro 504K replica		§ '18
☐ 'G-ADRY'	Mignet HM.14 Flying Flea	Fr c37	
☐ G-AEKV	Kronfeld Drone de Luxe		'36
☐ G-AGRU	Vickers Viking 1		'46
☐ G-APES	Vickers Vanguard 953C Merchantman	'62	
☐ G-APIM	Vickers Viscount 806		'58
☐ G-ASYD	BAC 111-475AM		'65
☐ G-BJHV	Voisin scale replica	Fr '07	
☐ G-LOTI	Bleriot XI replica	Fr '09	
☐ G-MJPB	Manuel Ladybird microlight		'82
☐ G-VTOL	HS Harrier T.52		'71
☐ 'B7270'	Sopwith Camel replica ✈ (G-BFCZ)		'18
☐ N2980	Vickers Wellington IA		'39
☐ WF372	Vickers Varsity T.1 [A]		'51
☐ WT859	Supermarine 544 nose		'56
☐ XA292	Slingsby Cadet TX.3 ✈		'52
☐ XD816	Vickers Valiant BK.1 nose		'56
☐ XJ571	DH Sea Vixen FAW.2		'58
☐ E-421	Hawker Hunter F.51		'56
☐ –	Abbott-Baynes Scud II (AAA)		'35
☐ –	BAC TSR-2 nose		'64
☐ –	BAC VC-10 nose		c62
☐ –	Curtiss D Pusher replica	US '09	
☐ –	Hawker Typhoon IA cockpit	c41	
☐ –	Hawker Typhoon IB cockpit	c41	
–	Hols der Teufel glider replica ✈ (FHQ)	Gr c33	
☐ –	Manuel Willow Wren ((BGA.162)		'34
☐ –	Roe I Biplane replica (BAPC.187)		'08
☐ –	Rogallo hang glider	US c76	
–	Santos-Dumont Demoiselle replica (BAPC.194)		'11
☐ –	Slingsby Falcon I replica ((FCZ)	c30	
☐ –	Slingsby Gull III glider ✈ (ATH)		'45
–	Slingsby Kite I glider ✈ (AHC)		'39

Nearby:
Airborne Forces Museum, *16 mls – see page 82.*
Central London, *16 miles.*
Imperial War Museum, *16 miles – see page 36.*
Royal Air Force Museum, *20 miles – see page 38.*
Science Museum, *16 miles – see page 42.*
Windsor Castle and Safari Park, *10 miles.*

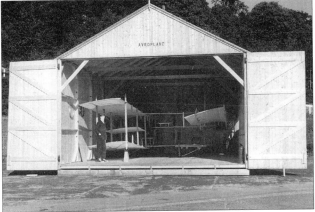

Top: The famed clubhouse at Brooklands housed Barnes Wallis' drawing office during the Second World War. The museum offers a rich mixture of classic cars and aircraft. Brooklands Museum

Above: A faithful replica of the Roe I Biplane and the shed that housed it at Brooklands. It is sited almost on the same spot as the original of 1908. Ken Ellis

FOULKES-HALBARD COLLECTION

Wannock, East Sussex

Address: Filching Manor, Jevington Road, Wannock, Polegate, East Sussex, BN26 5QA.

Telephone: 01323 487838 or'487124, Fax 01323 486331.

Where: On the unclassified road to Jevington from Wannock, East Sussex.

Open: Daily Easter to May Thursday to Sunday; May to October daily, 10.30am to 4.30pm. Other times by appointment.

By bus: Services from Eastbourne stop in Wannock.

By rail: Polegate 2 miles.

Tourist: Eastbourne 01323 411400, Fax 01323 649574.

Admission: £3 adult, Child/cons £2.

Facilities: Toilets/Parking/Cafe/Shop/Disabled/ Kids/All/Changes/Brochure.

There are many items at this venue queuing up for the accolade of 'star' not the least of which is the manor house itself which dates back to the 15th century. Aeronautically, the collection contains two aircraft – with the owner looking for more suitable examples – the Aldritt monoplane, a pioneer from

Ireland, and the Jupiter man-powered aircraft. Other items include a Rolls-Royce 'R' engine from the 1931 Schneider Trophy winning Supermarine team and a 1947 MetroVick Beryl. The car collection here is superb ranging from a 1904 Peugeot to the 1931 Alfa Romeo Mille Miglia. Also here is the original Campbell Bluebird K3 hydroplane record breaker of Sir Malcolm Campbell and a replica of the Bluebird K7 of Donald Campbell. Special events are frequently staged including go-cart racing on the Campbell Circuit.

Aircraft exhibits:

☐	–	Aldritt Monoplane (IAHC.2)	§ '10
☐	–	Halton Jupiter man-powered aircraft (BAPC.127)	'72

Nearby:

Bluebell Railway, *16 miles*.
Eastbourne, *4 miles*.
English Wine Centre, *2 miles*.
Hastings, *17 miles*.
Newhaven Fort, *8 miles – see page 77*.
Museum of D-Day Aviation and Shoreham Aerodrome, *20 miles – see page 76*.

Tucked in the rafters among the motor car treasures, the Jupiter man-powered aircraft. Ken Ellis

HURRICANE & SPITFIRE MEMORIAL BUILDING

RAF Manston, Kent

Address: RAF Manston, Ramsgate, Kent, CT12 5BS.

Telephone: 08143 823351, ext 2219.

Where: RAF Manston, follow the signs off the A253 Ramsgate road.

Open: Daily, May to September 1oam to 5pm, October to April 10am to 4pm.

By bus: Services to Ramsgate and Margate, 3 miles. By rail: Ramsgate 3 miles.

Tourist: Ramsgate 01843 591086.

Admission: Free. Donation much appreciated.

Facilities: Toilets/Parking/Cafe/Shop/Disabled/ All/Changes/Brochure.

Within the building can be found two pristine examples of the immortal Hurricane and Spitfire – both restored by the Medway Aircraft Preservation Society (see page 80). Also within is a wealth of material relating to Manston's role in the Battle of Britain and throughout the Second World War.

Aircraft exhibits:

☐	'BN230'	Hawker Hurricane II (LF751) [FT-A]	'44
☐	TB752	Supermarine Spitfire XVI [KH-Z]	'45

Nearby:

Canterbury, *12 miles.*

Dover, *16 miles.*

Kent Battle of Britain Museum, *18 miles – see page 74.*

Maritime Museum and Motor Museum, Ramsgate, *3 miles.*

Manston's impressive memorial building contains a Hurricane and a Spitfire in pristine condition, a host of artefacts and photographs and the appropriately named Merlin Cafetaria. Ken Ellis

KENT BATTLE OF BRITAIN MUSEUM

Hawkinge, Kent

Address: Aerodrome Road, Hawkinge Airfield, Folkestone, CT18 7AG.
Telephone: 01303 89340.
Where: Signposted off the A250 at Hawkinge, north of Folkestone.
Open: Daily Easter to September 30 10am to 5pm and October 1st-15th 11am to 4pm.
By bus: No 16 from Folkestone stops at entrance.
By rail: Folkestone 2 miles.
Tourist: Folkestone 01303 258594, Fax 01303 259754.
Admission: Adult £2.50, OAP £2, Child £1.50.
Facilities: Toilets/Parking/Cafe*/Shop/Disabled*/All/Changes/Brochure.

Within the museum is a renowned collection of artefacts charting every aspect of the Battle of Britain in Kent. A series of replica aircraft have been used to recreate scenarios and the majority of the items on show come from crash sites in the area. Displays take in uniforms, awards, airfield histories, weapons and much more. During the summer of 1995 Hangar No 2 was opened, increasing the floor space by 50%. This has allowed the First World War aircraft gallery to be established.

Aircraft exhibits:

☐	'D-3-340'	Grunau Baby 2 glider	Gr c36
☐	'P3208'	Hawker Hurricane replica (BAPC.63) [SD-T]	'40
☐	'N3289'	Sup Spitfire replica (BAPC.65) [DW-K]	'39
☐	'N3313'	Sup Spitfire replica (BAPC.69)	§ '39
☐	'P3059'	Hawker Hurricane replica (BAPC.64) [SD-N]	'40
☐	'425/17'	Fokker Dr I replica (BAPC.133)	Gr '17
☐	–	Fieseler Fi 103 (V-1) flying-bomb replica (BAPC.36)	Gr '45
☐	–	Messerschmitt Bf 109 replica (BAPC.66)	§ Gr '40
☐	–	Messerschmitt Bf 109 replica (BAPC.67)	Gr '40
☐	–	Messerschmitt Bf 109 replica (BAPC.74)	Gr '40
☐	–	RAF SE.5A replica (BAPC.167)	'18

Nearby:

Battle of Britain Memorial, *3 miles*.
Brenzett Aeronautical Museum, *16 miles* – see page 69.
Dover, *6 miles*.
Eurotunnel Exhibition, *5 miles*.
Folkestone, *3 miles*.
Hurricane and Spitfire Memorial Building, *18 miles* – see page 73.
Romney, Hythe & Dymchurch Railway, *10 miles*.

Clever use of replica aircraft and a huge array of engines and other parts recovered from Battle of Britain crash sites combine at Hawkinge. Ken Ellis

LASHENDEN AIR WARFARE MUSEUM

Headcorn Aerodrome, Kent

Address: Lashenden Aerodrome, Ashford, Kent, TN27 9HX.
Telephone: 01622 890226, Fax 01622 890876.
Where: Lashenden (or Headcorn) aerodrome, off the A274 south of Headcorn.
Open: Sundays and Bank Holidays 10.30am to 6pm from Easter until the end of October. Parties at other times by prior arrangement.
By bus: No 12 passes close to the museum.
By rail: Headcorn 2 miles.
Tourist: Ashford 01233 629165.
Admission: Free, donations welcomed.
Facilities: Toilets/Parking/Cafe/Shop/Changes/Brochure.

Lashenden served as an Advanced Landing Ground during the run-up to D-Day and the museum concentrates of the airfield's role. The airfield today is a thriving general aviation and parachute centre and activity can be seen from the museum enclosure to advantage. The small static aircraft park is supported by a huge array of artefacts, all carefully labelled and telling the tale of military aviation in Kent and life in wartime.

Aircraft exhibits:

☐ WZ450	DH Vampire T.11 nose [19]	'52
☐ WZ589	DH Vampire T.11 [19]	'53
☐ XN380	Westland Whirlwind HAS.7 [67]	US '61
☐ 84	Dassault Mystère IVA [8-NF]	Fr '55
☐ 63938	NA F-100F Super Sabre [11-MU]	US '56
☐ 100549	Focke-Achgelis Fa 330A-1 rotorkite	Gr '44
☐ –	Fieseler Fi 103R-IV piloted flying-bomb (BAPC 91)	Gr '45

Nearby:
Brenzett Aeronautical Museum, *14 miles –*
see page 69.
Hastings, *20 miles.*
Kent and East Sussex Railway, *8 miles.*
Romney, Hythe & Dymchurch Railway, *20 miles.*
Royal Engineers Museum, *16 miles –*
see page 77.

Lashenden's V-1 'Doodlebug' *may* be an original piloted 'Reichenberg' version. Ken Ellis

MUSEUM OF D-DAY AVIATION

Shoreham Airport, West Sussex

Address: Shoreham Aerodrome, Shoreham-by-
Sea, West Sussex, BN43 5FJ.
Telephone: 01374 971971.
Where: Shoreham Airport, access off the A27
east of Worthing.
Open: 11am to 5pm daily March to November.
By bus: Regular services into Shoreham-by-Sea.
By rail: Shoreham 1 mile.
Tourist: Worthing 01903 210022.
Admission: Adult £2.50, OAP £2, Child £1.50,
Family £5.
Facilities: Toilets/Parking/Cafe/Shop/Disabled/
All/Changes/Brochure.

Shoreham harbour played a pivotal role during the
D-Day operation and of course the entire south
coast was deeply involved in one form or another.
The museum serves to outline the effects of the
aerial armada on the region, its preparation, execu-
tion and aftermath. A vast collection of artefacts,
including a growing collection of military fire engines and an RAF air sea rescue boat. The museum
offers excellent views of the comings and goings of
aircraft from delightful Shoreham aerodrome. Special events, reunions and exhibitions are frequently
staged, including an annual fire engine rally.

Aircraft exhibit:

☐ 'MJ751' Sup Spitfire replica (BAPC.209) [DU-V] '44

Also:
Excellent cafe and viewing facilities within the
terminal building, including a terraced area under
the control tower. Within the terminal can be found
the Shoreham Aviation Heritage Centre, open
10.30am to 5pm daily, April to November, display-
ing pictures and artefacts from the aerodrome's
long history. A Beagle Pup 100 (G-AXTZ) is under
restoration locally for eventual display.

Nearby:
Bluebell Railway, *18 miles.*
Brighton, *6 miles.*
The Lavender Line, *18 miles.*
Newhaven Fort, *16 miles – see opposite.*
Tangmere Military Aviation Museum, *20 miles –
see page 78.*

Spitfire replica 'guarding' the aerodrome side of the Museum of D-Day Aviation at Shoreham. Ken Ellis

NEWHAVEN FORT

Newhaven, East Sussex

Address: Fort Road, Newhaven, East Sussex, BN9 9DL. **Telephone:** 01273 517622.
Where: Close to the mouth of the River Ouse, signposted in the town.
Open: 1st April to 1st October, daily 10.30am to 6.00pm. Also weekends in March and October and School Half Terms.
By bus: On the main bus route in the town.
By rail: Newhaven 1 mile.
Tourist: Seaford 01323 897426.
Admission: Adult £2.50, OAP £1.75, Child £1.50.
Facilities: Toilets/Parking/Cafe/Shop/Disabled*/Kids/All/Changes/Brochure.

Set in 10 acres of 1860s coastal defence fort, with underground tunnels and bunkers to explore. Excellent views of the coast and the incoming ferries from Dieppe. Displays on the Dieppe raid, D-Day, the Royal Observer Corps, the Home front and much more. Opened in August 1994 is a display by the Robertsbridge Aviation Society – see page 80. The aviation theme is expanding all the time.

Nearby:
Bluebell Railway, *12 miles.*
Brighton, *12 miles.*
Eastbourne, *10 miles.*
Foulkes-Halbard Collection, *8 miles – page 72.*
The Lavender Line, *10 miles.*

ROYAL ENGINEERS MUSEUM

Chatham, Kent

Address: Brompton Barracks, Chatham, Kent, ME4 4UG.
Telephone: 01634 406397, Fax 01634 822371.
Where: On North Road, off Gordon Road, off the A231 at Brompton north of Chatham.
Open: Open Monday to Thursday 10am to 5pm, Saturday and Sunday 11.30am to 5pm. Note not open on Fridays.
By bus: Several bus services pass nearby.
By rail: Gillingham 1 mile.
Tourist: Rochester 01634 843666.
Admission: Adult £2, Cons £1. Family tickets available.
Facilities: Toilets/Parking/Cafe/Shop/Disabled/All/Changes/Brochure.

The aviation content of the galleries here has increased recently, including a Harrier in an airfield 'hide'. There is much to interest the aviation enthusiast here including the medals etc of James McCudden and many other artefacts. The fascinating world of military engineering through the ages is shown through displays, vehicles and artefacts.

Aircraft exhibits:

☐ XT133	Agusta (Bell) Sioux AH.1	§ US '65	
☐ XZ964	HS Harrier GR.3 [D]	'80	
☐ –	Military balloon basket	c12	
☐ –	Vulcan hang-glider	c80	

Nearby:
Brands Hatch, *14 miles.*
Chatham Historic Dockyard, *2 miles.*
Fort Amherst, *1 mile.*
Lashenden Air Warfare Museum, *16 miles – see page 75.*
Medway Aircraft Preservation Society, *4 miles – see page 80.*
Motor Cycle Museum, Rochester, *3 miles.*
Shoreham Aircraft Preservation Society, *18 miles – see page 78.*
Sittingbourne & Kemsley Light Railway, *12 miles.*

SHOREHAM AIRCRAFT PRESERVATION SOCIETY
Shoreham, Kent

Address: High Street, Shoreham Village, Sevenoaks, Kent, TN14 7TB.
Telephone: 01959 524416.
Where: Off the A225 north of Sevenoaks.
Open: May to September Sundays only 10am to 5pm, or by prior arrangement.
By rail: Shoreham, walking distance.
Tourist: Sevenoaks 01732 450305.
Admission: Adult £1, children free.
Facilities: Toilets/Parking*/Cafe/Shop/Disabled*/ All/Changes/Brochure.

A superb museum based upon the society's extensive number of 'digs', all beautifully researched and presented. Large art gallery devoted to the work of local artist Geoff Nutkins.

Aircraft exhibit:

☐ TB885	Supermarine Spitfire XVI cockpit	§ '45

Nearby:
Central London, *16 miles.*
Chatham Historic Dockyard, *16 miles.*
Imperial War Museum, *16 miles – see page 36.*
Museum of Artillery, *16 miles – see page 37.*
Royal Engineers Museum, *18 miles – page 77.*
Science Museum, *16 miles – see page 42.*
Thameside Aviation Museum, *16 miles – see page 22.*

TANGMERE MILITARY AVIATION MUSEUM
Tangmere, West Sussex

Address: Tangmere Airfield, Chichester, West Sussex, PO20 6ES.
Telephone: 01243 775223.
Where: Signposted from the A27, nr Chichester.
Open: Daily 10am to 5.30pm from March to October and 10am to 4.30pm in February and November.
By bus: Chicester service passes the museum entrance.
By rail: Chichester 3 miles.
Tourist: Chichester 01243 775888, Fax 01243 539449.
Admission: Adult £3, OAPs £2.50, Child £1.
Facilities: Toilets/Parking/Cafe/Shop/Disabled/ Kids/All/Changes/Brochure.

An excellent museum, situated on the boundary of this former historic airfield. There is an external aircraft display area and four halls within charting 60 years of military aviation in Sussex. The Tangmere Hall concentrates on the history of the airfield from 1917–70. The Middle Hall covers a wide series of subjects, including the 'Dam Busters'. The Battle of Britain Hall contains a huge amount of material on the men and machines of the battle, including a major display on F/L J Nicolson VC. The recently completed Merston Hall includes replicas of a Hurricane and a Spitfire and two original world record breaking aircraft that achieved their fame flying from Tangmere. Special exhibitions are frequently staged, including the annual famous Aeromart.

Aircraft exhibits:

☐ 'L1679'	Hawker Hurricane replica		
☐	(BAPC.241) [JX-G]		'38
☐ 'BL924'	Sup Spitfire replica (BAPC.242) [AZ-G]		'42
☐ EE549	Gloster Meteor IV Special		'45
☐ WA984	Gloster Meteor F.8		'51
☐ WB188	Hawker P.1067		'51
☐ WK281	Supermarine Swift FR.5 [S]		'56
☐ 'XF314'	Hawker Hunter F.51 (E-412)		'56
☐ 19252	Lockheed T-33A 'T-Bird'	US	'51

Nearby:

Chichester, *3 miles.*

Goodwood House and Circuit, *3 miles.*

Hollycombe House Steam Collection, *16 miles.*

Museum of D-Day Aviation and Shoreham
Aerodrome, *20 miles – see page 76.*

City of Portsmouth, *18 miles.*

Below: **Hurricane replica in AEF markings inside the splendid aircraft hall at Tangmere.**
Bottom: **Latest exhibit at Tangmere is Swift FR.5 WK281 on loan from the RAF Museum.**
Both Ken Ellis

ALSO IN SOUTH EAST ENGLAND

THE MEDWAY AIRCRAFT PRESERVATION SOCIETY have their workshops at Rochester Airport, Kent. Currently work involves a Spitfire V for the RAF Museum, a Piper Tri-Pacer to flying condition and the restoration of the aerodynamic trials Short Sherpa prototype. The workshop facilities are open to the public on Sundays, Mondays and Wednesdays 9am to 1pm. Airport rules must be observed – the threshold of Runway 34 needs negotiating. SAE to Lewis Deal, 15 Amethyst Avenue, Chatham, Kent, ME5 9TX, 'phone or fax 01634 816492.

P G VALLANCE collection of aircraft at Charlwood in Surrey, close to Gatwick Airport, includes two Sea Princes, two Shackletons, a Pembroke C.1, Sea Hawk, Meteor T.7, Canberra PR.7, Gannet AEW.3 and others. Viewing by prior appointment, contact: Vallance By-Ways, Lowfield Heath Industrial Estate, Westfield Road, Lowfield Heath, Charlwood, Surrey, RH6 0BT. Telephone 01293 862915.

THE ROBERTSBRIDGE AVIATION SOCIETY have established their extensive and fascinating collection of airframes and artefacts at the Bush Barn, Robertsbridge, East Sussex. They have also staged an exhibition at Newhaven Fort (see page 77). Airframes held include a Tiger Moth under restoration, the nose sections of a Hunter F.2, Lightning F.3, Meteor T.7 and Sukhoi Su-7, plus a wide selection of engines and thousands of artefacts and illustrations. Open by appointment, contact: Philip Baldock, Upper Crabbe Cottage, Five Ashes, Mayfield, East Sussex, TN20 6HJ.

Part of a 'wartime life' exhibit at the Robertsbridge Aviation Society's Bush Barn site. Ken Ellis

SOUTHERN ENGLAND
Berkshire, Buckinghamshire, Hampshire, Isle of Wight, Oxfordshire

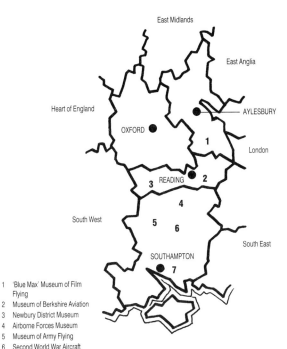

1 'Blue Max' Museum of Film
  Flying
2 Museum of Berkshire Aviation
3 Newbury District Museum
4 Airborne Forces Museum
5 Museum of Army Flying
6 Second World War Aircraft
  Preservation Society
7 Hall of Aviation Southampton

Southern Tourist Board
40 Chamberlayne Road, Eastleigh, Hampshire, SO5 5JH
Tel: 01703 620006 Fax: 01703 620010

AIRBORNE FORCES MUSEUM

Aldershot, Hampshire

Address: Browning Barracks, Aldershot, Hampshire, GU11 2DS.
Telephone: 01252 349619, Fax 01252 349203.
Where: Signposted off the A325 in Aldershot.
Open: Daily, 10am to 4.30pm. Special group visits by prior arrangement.
By bus: Several bus services pass close by.
By rail: Aldershot 1 mile.
Tourist: Fleet 01252 811151.
Admission: Adult £2, OAP/Child £1.
Facilities: Toilets/Parking/Cafe/Shop/Disabled/Kids/All/Changes/Brochure.

With a Douglas Dakota on show outside the museum and substantial elements of two assault gliders from the Second World War, the museum serves to chart the history of Britain's airborne forces and their many campaigns. Large series of displays including post-war campaigns, vehicles, equipment and personalities.

Aircraft exhibits:

☐ KP208	Douglas Dakota IV	US '44
☐ –	Airspeed Horsa II nose	'42
☐ –	GAL Hotspur II nose	'41

Nearby:
Brooklands Museum, *16 miles – see page 70.*
Hollycombe House Steam Collection, *12 miles.*
Mid-Hants Railway, *16 miles.*
Museum of Berkshire Aviation, *16 miles – see page 87.*
REME Museum, Arborfield, *14 miles.*
Second World War Aircraft Preservation Society, *14 miles – see page 89.*
Windsor Castle and Safari Park, *16 miles.*

'BLUE MAX' MUSEUM OF FILM FLYING

Wycombe Air Park, Buckinghamshire

Address: Wycombe Air Park, Marlow, Bucks, SL7 3DP.
Telephone: 01494 529432 or '449810 or Fax 01494 461236.
Where: Wycombe Air Park (or Booker), off the B482 south of High Wycombe.
Open: Open daily, 10am to 5pm.
By bus: Bus service from High Wycombe.
By rail: High Wycombe 3 miles.
Tourist: Marlow* 01628 483597. High Wycombe 01494 421892.
Admission: Adult £2.50, OAP/Child £1.50.
Facilities: Toilets/Parking/Shop/All/Changes/Brochure.

Run by Bianchi Aviation Film Services (BAFS), specialist film aviation service suppliers for many years, the museum is unique this side of the Atlantic. Aircraft and artefacts from a range of films are on show, including *Those Magnificent Men in Their Flying Machines*, *The Battle of Britain*, *Indiana Jones and the Last Crusade* and *The Blue Max*, from which the museum takes its name. Major changes carried out during the winter of 1994-95 have resulted in a series of set-pieces using 'star' aircraft and placing them in an even more vivid movie setting. Another very welcome move is allowing visitors to see restoration work on BAFS aircraft – perhaps readying them for a new film 'role' – and aircraft being worked on for other collectors and musuems. Please note that many of the aircraft are airworthy and used for film projects and other purposes and it may well be that not all of the aircraft in the following list are available at any one time.

Aircraft exhibits:

☐ EC-ACB	Miles Falcon	§ '36
☐ G-AWXZ	SNCAN SV-4C ✈	Bel '46
☐ G-AYFO	Bücker Bü 133C Jungmeister (N40BJ)	Gr '38
☐ G-AZTR	SNCAN SV-4C ✈	Bel '46
☐ G-BAAF	Manning-Flanders MF.1 replica	'12
☐ G-BLKZ	Pilatus P.2-05 ✈	Sws c50
☐ G-BPVE	Bleriot XI replica ✈	Fr '09
☐ G-BTBJ	Cessna 190B ✈	US c52
☐ G-BTZE	Yakovlev C-11	§ Ru c51
☐ LV-ZAU	Focke-Wulf Fw 44 Stieglitz	Gr c34
☐ N6268	Travel Air 2000	§ US '25
☐ 'B2458'	Sopwith Camel replica ✈ (G-BPOB) [R]	'17
☐ AR213	V-S Spitfire Ia ✈ (G-AIST) [PR-D]	'41
☐ 'MS821'	Morane Saulnier 'N' replica ✈ (G-AWBU)	Fr '14
☐ MV262	V-S Spitfire XIV (G-CCVV)	'45
☐ NJ695	Auster 4 (G-AJXV)	'44
☐ PL344	V-S Spitfire IX ✈ (G-IXCC)	§ '44
☐ TE476	V-S Spitfire XVI (G-XVIB)	§ '45
☐ TE517	V-S Spitfire IX (G-CCIX)	§ '45
☐ '143'	MS Alcyon (F-BLXV)	§ Fr '52
☐ '157'	MS.230 Et2 ✈ (G-AVEB)	Fr '49
☐ '422/15'	Fokker E.III replica ✈ (G-AVJO)	Gr '15
☐ –	Hulton hang-glider (BAPC.103)	'69
☐ –	Pilatus P.2 fuselage, film mock-up	Sws c50
☐ –	Waxflatter Ornithopter (BAPC.238)	c76
☐ –	Yakovlev Yak C-11	§ Ru c51

Also:

Wycombe Air Park is a busy light aviation, helicopter and gliding airfield and the tower building offers a good cafe and vantage point to see flying taking place. The aerodrome is also the home of Tiger Fly who undertake pleasure flights from the airfield using a Tiger Moth in Second World War camouflage – prior booking necessary.

Nearby:

Museum of Berkshire Aviation, *14 miles* – see page 87.
Railway Centre, Waddesdon, *18 miles.*
Windsor Castle and Safari Park, *12 miles.*

The MS.230 parasol has appeared in several films, including 'The Blue Max' when it played the role of the fateful 'German' prototype fighter in which the anti-hero eventually meets his end. Bill Hale

HALL OF AVIATION
Southampton, Hampshire

Address: Albert Road South, Southampton, SO1 1FR.
Telephone: 0703 635830.
Where: Close to Ocean Village and the Itchen Bridge, signed off the A36 in the southern part of the city centre.
Open: Daily except Mondays and over Christmas, 10am to 5pm (Tuesday to Saturday) and 2pm to 5pm (Sundays).
By bus: Several services.
By rail: Southampton Central 1 mile.
Tourist: 01703 221106, Fax 01703 631437.
Admission: Adult £3, OAP £2, Child £1.50.
Facilities: Toilets/Shop/Disabled/All/Brochure.

The area around Southampton and the Solent is steeped in aviation history and the hall illustrates this heritage vividly, being dominated by the Sandringham flying-boat which stands for the impressive machines that flew from the Solent to all points of the globe from the 1920s to the mid-1950s. Supermarine is synonymous with the area, the prototype Spitfire making its first flight from Southampton Airport in 1936. Airspeed, Avro, Britten Norman, de Havilland, Folland, Saunders-Roe and small concerns like Wight all have local connections and their stories are charted in the many displays.

Aircraft exhibits:

☐ G-ALZE	Britten Norman BN-1F		'51
☐ VH-BRC	Short Sandringham 4		'43
☐ N248	Supermarine S.6A		'29
☐ 'N546'	Wight Quadruplane replica (BAPC.164)		'16
☐ 'C4451'	Avro 504J replica (BAPC.210)		'17
☐ BB807	DH Tiger Moth (G-ADWO)		'35
☐ PK683	V-S Spitfire F.24		'46
☐ TG263	SARO SR.A1 jet flying-boat		'47
☐ WK570	DHC Chipmunk T.10 cockpit	Can	'52
☐ WM571	DH Sea Venom FAW.22		'54
☐ WZ753	Slingsby Grasshopper TX.1		'55
☐ XD235	Supermarine Scimitar F.1		'59
☐ XD596	DH Vampire T.11		§ '54
☐ XJ476	DH Sea Vixen FAW.1 nose		§ '57
☐ XK740	Folland Gnat F.1		'56
☐ XL770	SARO Skeeter AOP.12		'60
☐ XN246	Slingsby Cadet TX.3		'62
☐ –	Airwave hang glider (BAPC.215)		c78
☐ –	SUMPAC man-powered aircraft (BAPC.7)		'61

Nearby:
Isle of Wight, *16 miles (20 minutes by hydrofoil)*.
Maritime Museum and the Ocean Village Marina, *walking distance*.
Mid-Hants Railway, *20 miles*.
Museum of Army Flying, *20 miles, opposite*.
National Motor Museum, *6 miles*.

SUMPAC – Southampton University Man-Powered AirCraft, the UK's first such device to fly. Ken Ellis

Above: **SR.A1 flying-boat jet fighter, first flown on 16th July 1947. Intended as a means of providing air cover for the 'island-hopping' fight against Japan, it was overtaken by events.** Author's collection

Below: **Airspeed Horsa assault glider in 'just landed' pose at the Museum of Army Flying.** Ken Ellis

MUSEUM OF ARMY FLYING
Middle Wallop Airfield, Hampshire

Address: Middle Wallop, Stockbridge, Hampshire, SO20 8DY.
Telephone: 01980 674421, Fax 01264 781694.
Where: Middle Wallop Airfield, on the A343 south west of Andover.
Open: 10am to 4.30pm every day.
By bus: Hampshire No 7516 and the Sunday Rider No 9012 stop outside.
By rail: Andover 5 miles.
Tourist: Andover 01264 324320.
Admission: Adult £3.75, OAP £2.75, Child £2.25, Family £10.
Facilities: Toilets/Parking/Cafe/Shop/Disabled/ Kids/All/Changes/Brochure.

Army aviation is the oldest form of military flying in the UK and via its impressive display halls the museum tells the story from man-lifting kites and gas balloons through to the advent of the awesome new attack helicopter shortly to be chosen for today's Army Air Corps. The days of 'eyes for the guns' and the Austers and the 'silent messengers' of the Glider Pilot Regiment are given vivid full-size dioramas. The development of the helicopter is shown from the earliest experiments. The museum car park and the excellent cafe both afford superb views of the fixed wing and helicopter activity on Middle Wallop airfield, the headquarters of the Army Air Corps. Special exhibitions and events are frequently staged.

Aircraft exhibits:

☐ G-AXKS	Westland-Bell 47G-4A	US '69
☐ G-BVGZ	Fokker DR.I replica →	Gr '17
☐ 'B-415'	AFEE 10/42 'Rotajeep' replica (BAPC.163)	'42
☐ P-5	Hafner Rotachute AR.III	'42
☐ '5964'	Airco DH.2 replica (BAPC.112)	'16
☐ D7560	Avro 504K	'17
☐ 'N5195'	Sopwith Pup (G-ABOX)	'17
☐ N6985	DH Tiger Moth ((G-AHMN)	'39
☐ 'KJ351'	Airspeed Horsa II fuselage (BAPC.80)	'42
☐ TJ569	Auster 5 (G-AKOW)	'45
☐ TK777	GAL Hamilcar I fuselage	'44
☐ WJ358	Auster AOP.6 (G-ARYD)	'52
☐ WZ721	Auster AOP.9	'51
☐ XG502	Bristol Sycamore HR.14	'55
☐ XK776	ML Utility Mk 1	'55
☐ XL738	SARO Skeeter AOP.12	'58
☐ XL813	SARO Skeeter AOP.12	'59
☐ 'XM819'	E Percival Prospector	'58
☐ XP821	DHC Beaver AL.1	Can '62
☐ XP822	DHC Beaver AL.1	Can '62
☐ XP847	Westland Scout AH.1	'61
☐ XR232	Sud Alouette AH.2	Fr '60
☐ XR458	Westland Whirlwind HAR.10 [H]	US '63
☐ XT108	Agusta-Bell Sioux AH.1	US '66
☐ XT638	Westland Scout AH.1 [N]	'66
☐ A-533	FMA Pucara	Arg c76
☐ AE-406	Bell UH-1H Iroquois	US '72
☐ AE-409	Bell UH-1H Iroquois	US '72
☐ 111989	Cessna L-19A Bird Dog	US '51
☐ '243809'	WACO CG-4A Hadrian (BAPC.185) [10]	US c44
☐ –	Hafner R-II (BAPC.10)	Aust '32
☐ –	Slingsby Kite I → (ACH) [E]	'36
☐ –	Westland Scout cabin	c66

Nearby:

Hall of Aviation and city of Southampton, *20 miles, see page 84.*
Mid-Hants Railway, *20 miles.*
Newbury District Museum, *18 miles – page 88.*
Stonehenge, *18 miles.*

The Hafner Rotachute, a 'strap-on' rotorkite for airborne assault. Ken Ellis

MUSEUM OF BERKSHIRE AVIATION

Woodley, Berkshire

Address: Mohawk Way (off Bader Way), Woodley, near Reading, Berkshire, RG5 4UF.
Telephone: 01734 340712.
Where: At Woodley, east of Reading.
Open: Saturdays, Sundays and Bank Holidays March to October, 10.30am to 5pm. During May, June and July also open Wednesdays to Fridays 11.30am to 4pm.
By bus: Nos 63/65 come close to the museum.
By rail: Reading 2 miles.
Tourist: 01734 566226, Fax 01734 566719.
Admission: Adult £2, OAP/Child £1.
Facilities: Toilets/Parking/Cafe/Shop/Disabled/ All/Changes/Brochure.

The former airfield at Woodley, which is close to the site of the museum, was the home of the hallowed firms of Miles Aircraft and later Handley Page and the museum serves to highlight the history of the airfield and the aircraft flown and built there and of the history of aviation in the county. Restoration of the Herald, in the hands of the Herald Society, continues apace.

Aircraft exhibits:

☐	G-APWA	HP Herald 100	'59
☐	6W-SAF	Douglas C-47A Skytrain nose	US '42
☐	'L6906'	Miles Magister I (BAPC.44)	'39
☐	XJ389	Fairey Jet Gyrodyne	'47
☐	–	Broburn Wanderlust (BAPC.233)	'46
☐	–	Rogallo-type hang glider	c75

Nearby:
Airborne Forces Museum, *14 miles – see page 82.*
'Blue Max' Museum of Film Flying, *14 miles – see page 82.*
City of Reading, *3 miles.*
Second World War Aircraft Preservation Society, *18 miles – see page 89.*

Miles Magister trainer, honouring a hallowed local aircraft manufacturer at Woodley. Ken Ellis

NEWBURY DISTRICT MUSEUM

Newbury, Berkshire

Address: The Wharf, Newbury, Berks, RG14 5AS.
Telephone: 01635 30511.
Where: The Wharf, Newbury, signed in the centre of the town.
Open: Open April to September 10am to 5pm Mon/Tue/Thu/Fri and 1pm to 5pm Sundays and Bank Holidays. October to March from 10am to 4pm Mon/Tue/Thu/Fri and closed Sundays and Bank Holidays. Note, the Museum is closed every Wednesday – except school holidays.
By bus: Buses into Newbury from Reading.
By rail: Newbury, walking distance.
Tourist: Newbury 01635 30267, Fax 01635 519431.
Admission: Free.
Facilities: Shop/Disabled*/All/Brochure.

Using artefacts on loan from the British Balloon Museum and Library plus slides and other material, the museum shows the history of ballooning from 1783 to the present day. Other topics covered by displays in the museum include canals, crafts and industries costume, the civil war etc.

Aircraft exhibits:

☐	G-BBGZ	Cambridge hot air balloon basket	'73
☐	G-BHKR	Colt 14A Cloudhopper hot air balloon	'80
☐	–	Military Gas balloon basket	c41

Nearby:

Didcot Railway Centre, *16 miles.*
Museum of Berkshire Aviation, *20 miles –*
see page 87.

Also...

The British Balloon Museum and Library holds an annual 'inflation day' for historic balloons, near Newbury. SAE to: BBML, 75 Albany Road, Old Windsor, Berkshire, SL4 2QD.

The ballooning display at Newbury District Museum. Peter J Bish

SECOND WORLD WAR AIRCRAFT PRESERVATION SOCIETY

Lasham Aerodrome, Hampshire

Address: Bob Coles, 8 Barracane Drive, Crowthorne, Berkshire, RG11 7NU.

Where: Located to the east of the gliding headquarters, on the north side of Lasham aerodrome, near Alton.

Open: Open Sundays and Bank Holidays 10am to 6pm (or dusk if first) and other times by arrangement.

By rail: Alton 8 miles.

Tourist: Basingstoke 01256 817618.

Admission: Free, donations welcomed.

Facilities: Parking/Shop/Brochure.

A long-established preservation group with a large aircraft display park including two NATO types, a former Israeli Meteor and the only DHA Drover in the northern hemisphere. Interior displays cover recovered items from Second World War crash sites in the region. As well as the aircraft and artefact collection, the museum offers a commanding view of the intensive gliding activity on the airfield. Trial lessons are available from the Lasham Gliding Society building.

Aircraft exhibits:

☐ 'VH-FDT'	DHA Drover II (G-APXX)	Aus '51
☐ 4X-FNA	Gloster Meteor NF.13	'53
☐ VR192	Percival Prentice 1 (G-APIT)	'48
☐ WF137	Percival Sea Prince C.1	'50
☐ WH291	Gloster Meteor F.8	'51
☐ WV798	Hawker Sea Hawk FGA.6 [026]	'54
☐ XK418	Auster AOP.9	'56
☐ XM833	Westland Wessex HAS.3	US '60
☐ E-423	Hawker Hunter F.51	'56
☐ 22+35	Lockheed F-104G Starfighter	US '61

Nearby:

Airborne Forces Museum, *12 miles, see page 82.*
Hollycombe House Steam Collection, *14 miles.*
Museum of Berkshire Aviation, *20 miles – see page 87.*
City of Winchester, *15 miles.*

ALSO IN SOUTHERN ENGLAND

At **ROYAL NAVAL AIR STATION FLEETLANDS**, near Gosport, Hampshire, is a fine museum tracing the history of the base; included is a Sea Vixen FAW.1 and a Whirlwind HAS.7. Viewing is by prior arrangement, contact the Curator, RNAY Fleetlands Museum, Gosport, Hampshire, or telephone 01707 822351, ext 44391.

Glider's eye view of the Second World War Aircraft Preservation Society aircraft park at Lasham. Ken Ellis

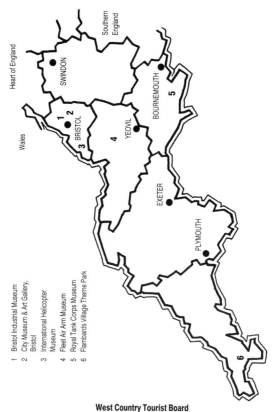

WEST COUNTRY
Avon, Cornwall, Devon, Dorset, Somerset, Wiltshire

Southern England

Heart of England

SWINDON

Wales

1
2
BRISTOL
3

YEOVIL

4

BOURNEMOUTH

5

EXETER

PLYMOUTH

6

1 Bristol Industrial Museum
2 City Museum & Art Gallery, Bristol
3 International Helicopter Museum
4 Fleet Air Arm Museum
5 Royal Tank Corps Museum
6 Flambards Village Theme Park

West Country Tourist Board
60 St David's Hill, Exeter, Devon, EX4 4SY
Tel: 01392 76351 Fax: 01392 420891

BRISTOL INDUSTRIAL MUSEUM

Bristol, Avon

Address: Prince's Wharf, Bristol, BS1 4RN.
Telephone: 0117 9251470, Fax 0117 9297318.
Where: On Prince's Wharf, south of the A4044 inner ring and well signed from the city centre.
Open: Tuesday to Sunday 10am to 5pm. Closed Mondays except Bank Holidays.
By bus: No 511 passes close. Any others to the city centre, then 10 minutes walk.
By rail: Temple Meads, 10 minutes walk.
Tourist: Bristol 0117 9260767, Fax 0117 297703.
Admission: Adult £1, Cons 50p, Children free.
Facilities: Toilets/Parking/Shop/Disabled/All/ Brochure.

As well as the Sycamore helicopter, there is a fabulous array of Bristol aero engines on show – many having been restored by the Rolls-Royce Heritage Trust, Bristol Branch – see page 99. Also here is a 'walk-through' engineering mock-up of Concorde. Within the museum are displays on the local docks and an excellent road transport section. Located on the 'Floating harbour' element of the River Avon, the museum offers superb views of the river and the buildings around.

Aircraft exhibit:

☐ XL829	Bristol Sycamore HR.14		'57

Nearby:
Avon Valley Railway, *5 miles.*
City of Bath, *12 miles.*
SS *Great Britain* and Maritime Heritage Centre, *10 minutes walk down the quayside.*
International Helicopter Museum, *20 miles – see page 97.*
City Museum and Art Gallery, *1 mile – see opposite.*

See overleaf.

CITY MUSEUM AND ART GALLERY

Bristol, Avon

Address: Queen's Road, Clifton, Bristol, BS8 1RL.
Telephone: 0117 9223571, Fax 0117 9222047.
Where: On the A4018 to the west of the city centre, near the University.
Open: Every day including Sundays, 10am to 5pm.
By bus: Many bus routes possible.
By rail: Temple Meads, short walk.
Tourist: Bristol 0117 9260767, Fax 0117 297703.
Admission: Adult £2, Cons £1, Children free.
Facilities: Toilets/Parking/Cafe/Shop/Disabled/ All/Changes/Brochure.

Suspended within the foyer of this delightful building is a Bristol Boxkite replica and there are other aviation artefacts on show, detailing aviation in Bristol. The remainder of the museum covers a wide range of topics, including Egyptology, the civil war, natural history etc.

Aircraft exhibit:

☐ –	Bristol Boxkite replica (BAPC.40)		'10

Nearby:
Avon Valley Railway, *5 miles.*
City of Bath, *12 miles.*
Bristol Industrial Museum, *1 mile – see opposite.*
SS *Great Britain* and Maritime Heritage Centre, *10 minutes walk down the quayside.*
International Helicopter Museum, *20 miles – see page 97.*

Also:
For both **Bristol** locations, **Bristol Balloons** offer pleasure flights, subject to weather throughout the year. Contact: Parklands Road, Bristol, BS3 2JW, or telephone 0117 9637858.

See overleaf.

Above: **Dominating the entrance hall of the City of Bristol Museum and Art Gallery is a Boxkite replica.**
Below: **Sycamore helicopter in among the aero engines at the Bristol Industrial Museum.** Both Ken Ellis

FLAMBARDS VILLAGE THEME PARK

Helston, Cornwall

Address: Clodgey Lane, Helston, Cornwall, TR13 0GA.

Telephone: Tel 01326 564093, Fax 01326 573344.

Where: Signed off the A3083 south of Helston, alongside RNAS Culdrose.

Open: Every day Easter to end of October 10am to 5pm. Last admission 3.30pm.

By bus: Western National stops within the museum.

By rail: Redruth 12 miles.

Tourist: On site* 01326 565431. Falmouth 01326 312300, Fax 01326 313457.

Admission: Adult £6.95, Child £6.25, Seniors (over 55) £4.50.

Facilities:
Toilets/Parking/Cafe/Shop/Disabled/Kids/All/Changes/Brochure.

The aeronautical collection here was previously known as the Cornwall Aero Park. Views of the fly-ing underway at the Royal Naval Air Station Culdrose are easily achieved from the museum. The theme park includes a wide range of entertainment and rides plus an Edwardian theme village.

Aircraft exhibits:

☐ G-BDDX	Whittaker Excalibur homebuild		'76
☐ WF122	Percival Sea Prince T.1 [575-CU]		
☐ WG511	Avro Shackleton T.4 nose		'52
☐ 'WG754'	Westland Dragonfly HR.5 (WG725) [912-CU]		US '52
☐ WK122	EE Canberra TT.18 [22]		'54
☐ WV106	Douglas Skyraider AEW.1 [427-C]	US '50
☐ XA870	Westland Whirlwind HAS.1	§ US '54
☐ XD332	Supermarine Scimitar F.1 [194-C]		'60
☐ XE368	Hawker Sea Hawk FGA.6 [200-J]		'55
☐ XG831	Fairey Gannet ECM.6 [396]		'56
☐ XN647	DH Sea Vixen FAW.2 [707-VL]		'61
☐ XP350	Westland Whirlwind HAR.10	US '62
☐ XS887	Westland Wessex HAS.1 [403-FI]	US '66
☐ XT427	Westland Wasp HAS.1 [606]		'65

Nearby:

Falmouth, *10 miles.*

Hayle Towans Railway, *10 miles.*

Lappa Valley Railway, *20 miles.*

Dragonfly HR.5 at Flambards Village Theme Park. John Uncles

FLEET AIR ARM MUSEUM

Yeovilton Airfield, Somerset

Address: RNAS Yeovilton, Ilchester, Somerset, BA22 8HT.

Telephone: 01935 840565, Fax 01935 840181

Where: Well signed off the A303 west of Wincanton.

Open: Every day (other than Xmas) March to October 10am to 5.30pm and November to February 10am to 4.30pm.

By bus: Regular services into Ilchester, 2 miles.

By rail: Yeovil 6 miles.

Tourist: Podimore* 01935 841302. Yeovil 01935 71279, Fax 01935 34065.

Admission: Adult £5.80, Child £3.30, Seniors £4.80.

Facilities: Toilets/Parking/Cafe/Shop/Disabled/ Kids/All/Changes/Brochure.

Dominating this large and vibrant museum is the incredible 'Carrier' exhibition in which visitors are 'flown' inside a Wessex helicopter onto the flight deck of an aircraft carrier after which they can roam the aircraft exhibits on the flight deck and go for a 'guided' tour of the 'island' – ending up at the bridge and 'FlyCo's' station. Complete with mannequin guide and soundtrack and special effects. As if this were not enough four galleries take the visitor through the entire history of naval aviation from the mud-splattered First World War section, to the bamboo of the Korean war exhibit, to the 'ski-jump' reconstruction in the vertical take-off section. Then there is the British Concorde prototype and the development aircraft that helped it on its way. A special gallery in the museum affords excellent views of the activity on the busy naval air station.

Nearby:

East Somerset Railway, *12 miles.*

Haynes Motor Museum, *2 miles.*

The impressive VTOL gallery includes an aircraft carrier 'ski-jump'. The Concorde exhibition lies beyond. FAAM

Above: 'MiG-15' amid the Korean war exhibit. Ken Ellis   Below: Inside the control room on board 'Carrier'. FAAM

Aircraft exhibits:

☐ 'G-ABUL'	DH Tiger Moth (XL717)	'40
☐ G-BSST	BAC/SNIAS Concorde 002	UK/Fr '69
☐ 8359	Short 184 fuselage	'15
☐ 'B6401'	Sopwith Camel replica (G-AWYY)	'17
☐ L2301	Supermarine Walrus I	'39
☐ L2940	Blackburn Skua I wreck	'39
☐ N1854	Fairey Fulmar II	'39
☐ 'N2078'	Sopwith Baby floatplane replica	'15
☐ 'N4389'	Fairey Albacore I (N4172) [4M]	'40
☐ 'N5492'	Sopwith Triplane replica (BAPC.111)	'17
☐ 'N6452'	Sopwith Pup replica (G-BIAU)	'17
☐ 'P4139'	Fairey Swordfish II (HS618)	'43
☐ AL246	Grumman Martlet I	US '40
☐ DP872	Fairey Barracuda II fuselage	'41
☐ EX976	NA Harvard IIA	US '41
☐ KD431	Vought Corsair IV [E2-M]	US '44
☐ KE209	Grumman Hellcat II	US '44
☐ LZ551/G	DH Sea Vampire I	'45
☐ NF389	Fairey Swordfish III	'45
☐ SX137	Supermarine Seafire F.17	'45
☐ VH127	Fairey Firefly TT.4	'47
☐ VR137	Westland Wyvern TF.1	'47
☐ WA473	Supermarine Attacker F.1 [102-J]	'51
☐ WG774	BAC 221 ogival wing research aircraft	'52
☐ WJ231*	Hawker Sea Fury FB.11 [115-O]	'50
☐ WN493	Westland Dragonfly HR.5	US '53
☐ WT121	Douglas Skyraider AEW.1	§ US '51
☐ WV856	Hawker Sea Hawk FGA.6	'54
☐ WW138	DH Sea Venom FAW.22 [227-Z]	'55

☐ XA127	DH Sea Vampire T.22 nose	'54
☐ XB446	Grumman Avenger ECM.6B	US '45
☐ XD317	Supermarine Scimitar F.1 [112]	'59
☐ XG900	Short SC.1	'57
☐ XJ314	Rolls-Royce Thrust Measuring Rig ('Flying Bedstead')	'53
☐ XK488	Blackburn Buccaneer S.1	'58
☐ XL503	Fairey Gannet AEW.3 [070-E]	'60
☐ XL580*	Hawker Hunter T.8M [723]	'58
☐ XN957	Blackburn Buccaneer S.1 [630-LM]	'63
☐ XP841	HP.115 delta research aircraft	'61
☐ XP980	Hawker P.1127	'63
☐ XS508	Westland Wessex HU.5	US '64
☐ XS527	Westland Wasp HAS.1	'63
☐ XS590	DH Sea Vixen FAW.2 [131-E]	'66
☐ XT482	Westland Wessex HU.5	US '66
☐ XT596	McDD Phantom FG.1	'66
☐ XT769	Westland Wessex HU.5 [823-CU]	US '66
☐ XV333	HS Buccaneer S.2B [234-H]	'66
☐ AE-422	Bell UH-1H Iroquois	US '74
☐ 'D.5397'	Albatros D.Va replica (G-BFXL)	Gr '17
☐ 'S.3398'	SPAD XIII replica (G-BFYO)	Fr '17
☐ '102 /17'	Fokker Dr I scale replica (BAPC.88)	Gr '17
☐ 15-1585	Yokosuka MXY-7 Ohka 11 suicide weapon (BAPC.58)	Ja '45
☐ 01420	MiG MiG-15bis / Lim-2 (G-BMZF)	Ru c55
☐ 155848	McDD F-4S Phantom [WT]	§ US '78
☐ 159233	HS AV-8A Harrier [33-CG]	'74
☐ –	Fairey IIIF fuselage frame	'27
☐ –	Short S.27 replica (BAPC.149)	§ '10

Supermarine Attacker on the flight deck of 'Carrier'. Fleet Air Arm Museum

INTERNATIONAL HELICOPTER MUSEUM

Weston-super-Mare, Avon

Address: Weston Airport, Locking Moor Road, Weston-super-Mare, Avon, BS22 8PP.
Telephone: 01934 635227, Fax 01934 822400.
Where: On the A371 east of Weston and well signposted.
Open: Daily October to March 10am to 4pm, April to September 10am to 6pm.
By bus: Helibus 126, 826 and 827 from Weston sea front.
By rail: Milton Halt, 1 mile.
Tourist: Weston-super-Mare 01934 626838, Fax 01934 612006.
Admission: Adult £3, OAP £2.50, Child £2, Family ticket £8.
Facilities: Toilets/Parking/Cafe/Shop/Disabled/All/Changes/Brochure.

Further expansion plans are underway at the popular museum, including a display hall and further exhibits. The truly international flavour continues with the acquisition of the an awesome Mil 'Hind' Soviet tankbuster, while UK achievements are not forgotten with the arrival of Westland's world record breaking Lynx G-LYNX. There is an extensive workshop with several helicopters always receiving attention – the public can watch progress. Inside displays include the history of helicopters, the story of Westland Helicopters, drone helicopters and two man-powered helicopter exhibits. 'Open Cockpit' days are held every second Sunday in the month, March to October and the annual 'HeliDays' fly-in is held on the Weston Sea Front each July. The museum also stages occasional 'Engineering Days' offering conducted tours of the workshop.

☐ D-HMQY	Bolkow Bo 102 Helitrainer	Gr '60
☐ F-BTRP	Sud Super Frelon	Fr '67
☐ G-ACWM	Cierva C.30A (Avro)	Sp '35
☐ G-ANFH	Westland Whirlwind Srs 1	§ US '54
☐ G-ANJV	Westland Whirlwind Srs 3	§ US '54
☐ G-AODA	Westland Whirlwind Srs 3	§ US '55
☐ G-AOUJ	Fairey Ultra Light Helicopter	§ '56
☐ G-ARVN	Servotec Grasshopper II	§ '62
☐ G-ASCT	Bensen B.8M gyrocopter	§ US '62
☐ G-ASHD	Brantly B.2A	§ US '63
☐ G-ASOL	Bell 47D-1	§ US '62
☐ G-ASTP	Hiller UH-12C	US '61
☐ G-ATBZ	Westland Wessex 60 Srs 1	§ US '66
☐ G-AVKE	Thruxton Gadfly HDW-1	§ '67
☐ G-AVNE	Westland Wessex 60 Srs 1	US '67
☐ G-AWRP	Cierva Rotorcraft Grasshopper III	§ '69
☐ G-AXFM	Cierva Rotorcraft Grasshopper III rig	§ '70
☐ G-AYNP	Westland Whirlwind Srs 3	§ US '59
☐ G-AZAU	Cierva Rotorcraft Grasshopper III rig	§ c71
☐ G-AZBY	Westland Wessex 60 Srs 1	§ US '71
☐ G-AZYB	Bell 47H-1	§ US '56
☐ G-BAPS	Campbell Cougar	§ '73
☐ G-BGHF	Westland WG.30-100	'79
☐ G-HAUL	Westland WG.30-TT300	'86
☐ G-LYNX	Westland Lynx 800	'79
☐ G-OAPR	Brantly B.2B ✈	§ US '65
☐ G-48-1	Bristol Sycamore 3	§ '51
☐ VR-BEU	Westland Whirlwind Srs 3	§ US '54
☐ 5N-ABW	Westland Widgeon 2	§ '57
☐ VZ962	Westland Dragonfly HR.1	§ US '51
☐ WG719	Westland Dragonfly HR.5 (G-BRMA)	§ US '52
☐ XA862	Westland Whirlwind HAS.1	US '52
☐ XD163	Westland Whirlwind HAR.10 [X]	US '54
☐ XE521	Fairey Rotodyne Y sections	'57
☐ XG452	Bristol Belvedere HC.1 (G-BRMB)	'60
☐ XG462	Bristol Belvedere HC.1 nose	§ '61
☐ XG547	Bristol Sycamore HR.14 (G-HAPR)	'56
☐ XG596	Westland Whirlwind HAS.7	§ US '57
☐ XL811	SARO Skeeter AOP.12	'58
☐ XM330	Westland Wessex HAS.1	US '59
☐ XP165	Westland Scout AH.1	§ '60 '60
☐ XP404	Westland Whirlwind HAR.10	§ US
☐ XS149	Westland Wessex HAS.3 [661-GL]	US '63
☐ 'XS463'	Westland Wasp HAS.1 (XT431)	'64
☐ XT148	Agusta-Bell Sioux AH.1	§ US '65
☐ XT443	Westland Wasp HAS.1 [422]	'66

☐ XT472	Westland Wessex HU.5 [XC]	US '66
☐ XW837	Westland Lynx 1-06	§ '70
☐ ZE477	Westland Lynx 3	'84
☐ 622	Piasecki HUP-3 Retreiver	US '54
☐ 9147	Mil Mi-4 'Hound'	Ru c58
☐ S-881	Sikorsky S-55C	§ US '54
☐ S-882	Sikorsky S-55C	§ US '54
☐ S-886	Sikorsky S-55C	§ US '54
☐ S-887	Sikorsky S-55C	§ US '54
☐ FR-108	Sud Djinn [CDL]	§ Fr '59
☐ 96+26	Mil Mi-24 'Hind-D'	Ru c77
☐ 05	WSK SM-2	Pol '61
☐ 2007	Mil Mi-1 (SM-1)	Ru '59
☐ 66-16579	Bell UH-1H Iroquois	US '67
☐ RG-05	Westland Lynx static rig	§ c70
☐ –	Westland Lynx 3 mock-up	'84
☐ –	Westland WG.30-300 rig	'84
☐ –	Murray Helicopter (BAPC.60)	§ '52
☐ –	Watkinson CG-4 Cyclogyroplane (BAPC.128)	'73
☐ –	Westland WG-33 mock-up (BAPC.153)	§ '78
☐ –	Bensen B.6 gyroglider (BAPC.212)	§ US c59
☐ –	Cranfield Vertigo man-powered helicopter (BAPC.213)	'80

Nearby:

Bristol Industrial Museum, City of Bristol Museum and others, *20 miles – see page 91*.
Somerset Railway, *1 mile*.

Above: **View of the IHM workshops, Widgeon in the foreground.**
Below: **Eastern** *bloc* **pair, Mi-1 and SM-2.** Both Ken Ellis

ROYAL ARMOURED CORPS AND ROYAL TANK REGIMENT TANK MUSEUM

Bovington, Dorset

Address: Bovington, Dorset, BH20 6JG.
Telephone: 01929 462721 or 09129 463953
(recorded message), Fax 01929 405360.
Where: Signposted from the A352 north of Wool.
Open: Open daily (with some exceptions) 10am
to 5pm.
By bus: Local services stop nearby.
By rail: Wool 2 miles.
Tourist: Wareham 01929 552740.
Admission: Adult £5, OAP £3.50, Child £3, family
ticket £12.
Facilities: Toilets/Parking/Cafe/Shop/Disabled/
Kids/All/Changes.

Over 200 armoured fighting vehicles of many
nationalities are on display, plus a huge amount of
supporting material. The Hamilcar transport glider
section will be used as a centre-piece with a Tetrar-
ch air portable tank. A Skeeter helicopter 'hovers'
above the tracked exhibits.

Aircraft exhibits:

☐ TK718	GAL Hamilcar I fuselage	'45
☐ XM564	SARO Skeeter AOP.12	'60

Nearby:
City of Bournemouth, *16 miles.*
Dorchester, *10 miles.*

ALSO IN THE WEST COUNTRY

**ROLLS-ROYCE HERITAGE TRUST. The Bristol
Branch** have established an astounding collection
of aero engines, centred on a former test shell
building within the Rolls-Royce plant at Filton, Bristol, Avon. Visits are by prior permission only, and
well worth it. Contact: Peter Pavey, AITD (GP2/1),
Rolls-Royce plc, PO Box 3, Filton, Bristol BS12
7QE.

The **SCIENCE MUSEUM Air Transport Collection and Storage Facility** is at Wroughton airfield,
near Swindon, Wiltshire. Housed here is a large
collection of airliners of all sizes, plus other large
items such as agricultural machinery, cars and lor-
ries. Sadly, the number of opportunities for the
public to inspect this fine collection is pitifully
small. Contact 01793 814466.

The **SEA VIXEN SOCIETY** keep DH Sea Vixen
FAW.2 XJ580 on public view on the B3059 Somerford Road, at the entrance to the Somerford Road
Retail Park, near MFI in Christchurch, Dorset. A
plaque explains that the Sea Vixen is a tribute to
aviation history in Christchurch 1932-1962 and that
it was presented by Troika Developments on 28th
April, 1985.

YORKSHIRE AND HUMBERSIDE
Humberside, North Yorkshire, South Yorkshire, West Yorkshire

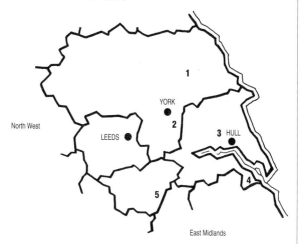

1   Eden Camp
2   Yorkshire Air Museum
3   Museum of Army Transport
4   NATO Aircraft Museum
5   South Yorkshire Aircraft
    Museum

Yorkshire and Humberside Tourist Board
312 Tadcaster Road, York, YO2 2HF
Tel: 01904 707961   Fax: 01904 701414

EDEN CAMP MODERN HISTORY THEME MUSEUM

Old Malton, North Yorkshire

Address: Malton, North Yorkshire, YO17 0SD.
Telephone: 01653 697777, Fax 01653 698243.
Where: On the A64 York to Scarborough road, north of Malton, near the junction with the A169. Signposted.
Open: Daily 10am to 5pm from February 14 to December 23, last admission 4pm. January to February weekdays only.
By bus: Local services, enquire via museum or local TIC.
By rail: Malton, 1 mile.
Tourist: Malton 01653 600048.
Admission: Adult £3, OAP/child £2.
Facilities:
Toilets/Parking/Cafe/Shop/Disabled/Kids/All/Changes/Brochure.

Once a prisoner of war camp, now an award-winning museum and theme park. Through its series of barrack-type huts, the museum uses extensive and detailed dioramas to tell the story of the second World war with heavy emphasis on the 'home front'. Major campaigns, at sea, on the ground and in the air, are explained in a vivid manner. There is a choice of 'Mess' to eat in, a cinema, even a period war news reading room. Three replica aircraft are displayed and there is a growing collection of operational military vehicles including a T-34 tank and an M16 half-track.

Aircraft exhibits:

☐	'P2793'	Hawker Hurricane replica (BAPC.236) [SD-M]	'40
☐	'AA908'	Supermarine Spitfire replica (BAPC.230) [UM-W]	'41
☐	–	Fieseler Fi 103 (V-1) flying-bomb replica	Gr '45

Nearby:
National Railway Museum, *17 miles.*
North Yorkshire Moors Railway, *16 miles.*
Scarborough, *20 miles.*
City of York, *17 miles.*
Yorkshire Air Museum, *17 miles – see page 105.*

Hurricane replica 'flying' above a Scammel recovery vehicle and a Spitfire replica at Eden Cam's entrance.
Eden Camp

MUSEUM OF ARMY TRANSPORT
Beverley, Humberside

Address: Flemingate, Beverley, North Humberside, HU17 0NG.

Telephone: 01482 860445 Fax 01482 866459.

Where: In Flemingate, Beverley, well signed within the town, close to the Minster.

Open: 10am to 5pm every day, closed December 24-26.

By bus: Regular services from Hull to Beverley.

By rail: Beverley Minister, walking distance.

Tourist: Beverley 01482 867430 or '883898, Fax 01482 883913.

Admission: Adult £3.50, OAP £2, Child £1.50, Family £8.50.

Facilities: Toilets/Parking/Cafe/Shop/Disabled/ Kids/All/Changes/Brochure.

Drive into the capacious car park of the museum and one item dominates the external displays at Flemingate – the only surviving Blackburn Beverley transport. This huge airlifter is not only an exhibit but serves as an exhibition hall! Within are displays on aerial despatch and on the huge task of moving the aircraft on to site and its restoration. The cockpit is occasionally open for inspection. Within the extensive museum building can be found many of the museum's 211 vehicles, including military locomotives, many of which are set in full-scale dioramas. There is also an extensive aircraft model collection set in its own 'house'.

Aircraft exhibit:
☐ XB259   Blackburn Beverley C.1   '55

Nearby:
Beverley Minster and town, *walking distance*.
Humber Bridge and Viewing Area, *9 miles*.
City of Kingston upon Hull, *8 miles*.

Below: **The Beverley dominates the exterior of the Museum of Army Transport.**
Above: **It also serves as an exhibition hall!** Both Ken Ellis

NATO AIRCRAFT MUSEUM

New Waltham, Humberside

Address: Grimsby-Cleethorpes Aircraft Preservation Group, 31 Montgomery Road, Cleethorpes, Humberside, DN35 9JG.
Where: Peak's Top Farm, New Waltham, south of Grimsby.
Open: Tuesday to Saturday 10am to 5pm.
By rail: Cleethorpes 3 miles.
Tourist: Cleethorpes 01472 200220, Fax 01472 601404.
Admission: Free, donations appreciated.
Facilities: Toilets/Parking/Cafe*/Changes/ Brochure.

Operated by the Grimsby-Cleethorpes Aircraft Preservation Group and previously known as the Museum of Weapons Technology, a growing collection of NATO 'hardware' is being assembled. Latest acquisition is a SAAB Draken from Denmark.

Aircraft exhibits:

☐ XR757	EE Lightning F.6 nose	'65
☐ XR770	EE Lightning F.6 [AA]	'66
☐ XS416	EE Lightning T.5	'64
☐ XS457	EE Lightning T.5 nose	'65
☐ A-011	SAAB A.35XD Draken	Swn '69
☐ 22+57	Lockheed F-104G Starfighter	US '62

Nearby:

Grimsby and Cleethorpes, *3 miles.*
Humber Bridge and Viewing Area, *20 miles.*
City of Kingston upon Hull, *20 miles.*
Lincolnshire Coast Light Railway, *3 miles.*

Latest exhibit at the NATO Air Museum is a SAAB Draken previously in service with the Royal Danish Air Force. via Chris Brydges

SOUTH YORKSHIRE AVIATION MUSEUM

Firbeck, South Yorkshire

Address: Ian Kingsnorth, South Yorkshire Aviation Society, 21 Broom Grove, Rotherham, South Yorkshire, S60 2TE.
Telephone: 01709 372821.
Where: At Home Farm, off the A364 Maltby to East Retford road, north of Firbeck village.
Open: Open every Sunday and Bank Holidays 10am to 5pm and at other times by arrangement.
By rail: Worksop 6 miles.
Tourist: Worksop 01909 501148, Fax 01909 501611.
Admission: Free, donations welcomed.
Facilities: Toilets/Parking/Cafe*/Shop/Disabled/ All/Changes/Brochure.

A lovely setting for a pleasing museum, once the site of the officers' mess of RAF Firbeck. As well as a wide variety of airframes on display in the aircraft park, there is an extensive aero engine collection, ranging from a Liberty of 1918 to the Pegasus that lifts and powers the Harrier. Also a large radio and radar equipment display, uniforms and flying clothing and a wide array of items from aviation archaeology 'digs' in the region.

Aircraft exhibits:

☐ G-ALYB	Auster 5	§ '44
☐ 'A4850'	RAF SE.5A scale replica (BAPC.176)	'18
☐ WA662	Gloster Meteor T.7	'50
☐ WM267	Gloster Meteor NF.11	'53
☐ WP255	DH Vampire NF.10 nose	'51
☐ WW388	Percival Provost T.1 [O-F]	'54
☐ XD528	DH Vampire T.11 pod	'54
☐ XE650	Hawker Hunter FGA.9 nose	'56
☐ XE935	DH Vampire T.11 [30]	'55
☐ XH584	EE Canberra T.4 nose	'55
☐ XM561	SARO Skeeter AOP.12	'59
☐ XN597	Hunting Jet Provost T.3 nose	'61
☐ XP190	Westland Scout AH.1	'62
☐ XP557	Hunting Jet Provost T.4	'62
☐ XS897	EE Lightning F.6	'66
☐ E-424	Hawker Hunter F.51	'56
☐ –	CASA 2-111 (He 111H) nose	Gr c53
☐ –	DHC Chipmunk T.10 cockpit	Can c52
☐ –	DH Vampire FB.5 nose	c50
☐ –	Hunting Jet Provost nose	c61

Nearby:

City of Doncaster, *12 miles.*
National Mining Museum, Bevercotes, *12 miles.*
Cities of Rotherham (16 miles) and Sheffield (20 miles).

A view of the aircraft park at Firbeck, Vampire T.11 and Jet Provost T.4. Ken Ellis

The South Yorkshire Aviation Museum contains an impressive selection of artefacts as well as airframes. Ken Ellis

YORKSHIRE AIR MUSEUM

Elvington, North Yorkshire

Address: Elvington, York, YO4 5AT.
Telephone: 01904 608595, Fax 01904 608246.
Where: Signed from the A64 southern York ring road, at the A64/A166/A1079 junction.
Open: Weekdays 10.30am to 4pm, weekends and Bank Holidays 10.30am to 5pm. Other times by arrangement.
By rail: York 5 miles.
Tourist: York 01904 620557, Fax 01904 620576.
Admission: Adult £3, OAP/Child £2.
Facilities: Toilets/Parking/Cafe/Shop/Disabled/All/Changes/Brochure.

Set around the former watch tower of RAF Elvington, the Yorkshire Air Museum has rapidly developed an impressive image. The watch tower has been carefully restored to its days when it was a Second World War base for Handley Page Halifaxes and although it looks out on to an apron of aircraft from a different era, is rich in atmosphere. All around wartime buildings have been restored, including the excellent NAAFI. The main display hall includes a close view of work in progress on the Halifax reconstruction project and outside the hangar that will contain the aircraft when finished is taking shape. In another workshop can be found the Night Fighter Preservation Team's superb DH Mosquito project, which is normally viewable at weekends. One of the display halls is devoted to the extensive Barnes Wallis collection, including much personal memorabilia and a fascinating display on the Swallow swing-wing experiments. Other displays include aero engines, the air gunners room and the life and times of Robert Blackburn.

Nearby:

Castle Howard, *14 miles.*
Eden Camp, *16 miles – see page 101.*
National Railway Museum, *5 miles.*
Real Aeroplane Company, *12 miles – see page 106.*
City of York, *5 miles.*

Lightning F.6 inside the main aircraft hall at the Yorkshire Air Museum. Steve Hague

Aircraft exhibits:

☐ 'G-AFFI'	Mignet HM.14 *Flying Flea* (BAPC.76)	Fr '36
☐ 'F943'	RAF SE.5A replica (G-BKDT)	'18
☐ 'H1968'	Avro 504K replica (BAPC.42)	§ '17
☐ HJ711	DH Mosquito NF.II [VI-C]	'43
☐ 'LV907'	HP Halifax II (HR792) [NP-F]	'43
☐ 'TJ704'	Beagle Terrier 2 (G-ASCD) [JA]	'48
☐ VV901	Avro Anson T.21	§ '49
☐ WH846	EE Canberra T.4	'54
☐ WG718	Westland Dragonfly HR.3	§ US '52
☐ WH991	Westland Dragonfly HR.3	§ US '53
☐ WS788	Gloster Meteor NF.14 [Z]	'54
☐ WX788	DH Venom NF.3	§ '54
☐ XD453	DH Vampire T.11	'54
☐ XL231	HP Victor K.2	'62
☐ XL572	Hawker Hunter T.7 (G-HNTR) [83]	'58
☐ XN974	HS Buccaneer S.2	'64
☐ XP640	Hunting Jet Provost T.4 [D]	'62
☐ XS903	EE Lightning F.6	'66
☐ 21417	Lockheed CT-133 Silver Star	US c54
☐ QA-10	Hawker Hunter FGA.78	'57
☐ –	EE Canberra nose	c54
☐ –	Hunting Jet Provost T.3 nose	c60

☐ –	RAF BE.2c replica (BAPC.41)	§ '16
☐ –	Blackburn Mercury replica (BAPC.130)	§ '12
☐	WACO CG-4A Hadrian fuselage (BAPC.157)	§ '43
☐ –	Messerschmitt Bf 109G replica (BAPC.240)	Gr '41

ALSO IN YORKSHIRE AND HUMBERSIDE

At **BREIGHTON** aerodrome (east of Selby between the villages of Bubwith and Breighton) the **Real Aeroplane Company** are busy establishing a museum of light aviation with construction of a display hall scheduled to start in late 1995. Presently, guided tours of the workshop and hangars are possible by prior arrangement. A series of fly-ins are also staged. Contact: The Real Aeroplane Company, The Aerodrome, Breighton, near Selby, North Yorks or telephone 01757 289065.

Above: **Local product, Buccaneer S.2, with Flying Flea behind.** Ken Ellis
Below: **Work underway on the ambitious Halifax project.** Steve Hague

SCOTLAND

Borders, Central Scotland, Dumfries & Galloway, Fife, Grampian, Highlands,
The Islands, Lothian, Strathclyde, Tayside

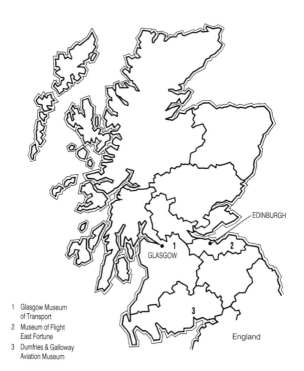

EDINBURGH

GLASGOW

England

1 Glasgow Museum
   of Transport
2 Museum of Flight
   East Fortune
3 Dumfries & Galloway
   Aviation Museum

Scottish Tourist Board
23 Ravelston Terrace, Edinburgh, EH4 3EU
Tel: 0131 3322433, Fax: 0131 3431513

DUMFRIES AND GALLOWAY AVIATION MUSEUM

Dumfries, Dumfries and Galloway

Address: David Reid, Chairman, 11 Ninian Court, Lochside, Dumfries.
Telephone: 01387 256680.
Where: Within the Heathhall Industrial Estate, on the former airfield, off the A701 to the north of the town.
Open: Saturdays and Sundays 10am to 5pm Easter to October, or by prior arrangement.
By bus: Service to Heathhall from Dumfries.
By rail: Dumfries 3 miles.
Tourist: Dumfries 01387 253862.
Admission: Adult £1.50, Child 75p.
Facilities: Toilets/Parking/Shop/Disabled*/ All*/Changes/Brochure.

Run by the Dumfries and Galloway Aviation Group, this is the only private aviation museum in Scotland. Using the airfield's former watch tower as its centre piece, there is also an aircraft display park. With respect to the airframes, the magic of the museum is to be found within the many intriguing displays inside the watch tower, including life on the RAF station during the Second World War, the 'fruits' of many local aviation archaeology excavations and much more.

Aircraft exhibits:

☐ P7540	Supermarine Spitfire IIA	§ '41
☐ AD540	Supermarine Spitfire V wreck	§ '41
☐ WA576	Bristol Sycamore 3	'51
☐ WD377	DHC Chipmunk T.10	§ Can '51
☐ WJ880	EE Canberra T.4 nose	'55
☐ WJ903	Vickers Varsity T.1 nose	'53
☐ WL375	Gloster Meteor T.7(mod)	'52
☐ WZ866	DHC Chipmunk T.10	§ Can '53
☐ XD547	DH Vampire T.11 [Z]	'54
☐ FT-36	Lockheed T-33A 'T-Bird'	US '55
☐ 318	Dassault Mystère IVA [8-NY]	Fr '55
☐ 42163	NA F-100D Super Sabre	US '54
☐ 68-0060	GD F-111E cockpit	US '68
☐ –	DH Venom nose	c51

Nearby:
Castle Douglas, *16 miles*.
Dumfries, *3 miles*.

See overleaf.

One of the treasure trove galleries within the watch tower at Dumfries. Ken Ellis

Vertigo-ridden views from the watch tower at Dumfries. **Above:** T-33A, Mystère, Sycamore and Meteor.
Below: Close-up of the F-100 Super Sabre 'Miss Kirsty'. Both Ken Ellis

MUSEUM OF TRANSPORT

Glasgow, Strathclyde

Address: Kelvin Hall, 1 Bunhouse Road, Glasgow, G3 8DP.
Telephone: 0141 3311854, Fax 0141 3052692.
Where: To the north west of the city centre, close to the Art Gallery and Museum.
Open: Weekdays 10am to 5pm and Sunday 11am to 5pm.
By bus: Several services available.
By rail: Glasgow Central 2 miles. Kelvin Hall underground.
Tourist: Glasgow 0141 2044400.
Admission: Free.
Facilities: Toilets/Cafe/Shop/Disabled/All/ Changes/Brochure.

Within a large display of cars, coaches – motorised and horse drawn, locomotives, trams and fire appliances can be found the pioneering Kay Gyroplane. Additional displays include Scottish made cars – where the Kay can be found – the Clyde room full of impressive ship models, a full-scale railway station platform and a Scottish street reconstruction of around 1938.

Aircraft exhibits:

☐ G-ACVA	Kay Gyroplane	'34
☐ –	Pilcher Hawk replica (BAPC.48)	§ 1896

Nearby:

City of Glasgow, use the underground network.
Greenock, *20 miles*.

The Kay Gyroplane can be found among the Scottish-built cars in Glasgow's Museum of Transport. Charles McKay

NATIONAL MUSEUMS OF SCOTLAND – MUSEUM OF FLIGHT

East Fortune Airfield, Lothian

Address: East Fortune Airfield, North Berwick, Lothian, EH39 5LF.

Telephone: 01620 88308, Fax 01620 88355.

Where: Signed off the A1, off the B1347 near East Linton.

Open: 10.30am to 5pm seven days a week April 1 to September 30. Parties at other times by appointment.

By rail: Drem 3 miles.

Tourist: Edinburgh 0131 5571700.

Admission: Adult £2, OAP/Child £1.

Facilities: Toilets/Parking/Cafe/Shop/Disabled/ Kids/All/Changes/Brochure.

East Fortune airfield was the departure point for the R34 airship on its historic Atlantic crossing of 1919. The entire airfield has been declared an historic monument, including buildings dating back to the First World War. There are over 30 aircraft on display ranging from a Falklands veteran Vulcan to a pair of MiG-15s. There is an exceptional display on air traffic control, a rocketry exhibition, a wide selection of aero engines and a space gallery. A continual, and fascinating, theme throughout the museum is the nature of flight and how man flies. Special exhibitions and occasion special events are held.

Nearby:
City of Edinburgh, *20 miles.*
Myreton Motor Museum, *5 miles.*

One of a pair of MiG-15s at the Museum of Flight, this one served with the Czechoslovakian Air Force. Steve Hague

The protoype Bulldog, built by Beagle at Shoreham, Sussex, in 1969. The type went into production at Prestwick with Scottish Aviation. *Alan Curry*

Aircraft exhibits:

☐ G-ACYK	Spartan Cruiser III fuselage	'34
☐ G-AFJU	Miles Monarch	§ '38
☐ G-AGBN	GAL Cygnet II	'40
☐ G-AHKY	Miles M.18-2	'39
☐ G-ANOV	DH Dove 6	'54
☐ G-AOEL	DH Tiger Moth	'40
☐ G-ARCX	Gloster Meteor Mk 14	'52
☐ G-ARTJ	Bensen B.8M gyrocopter	US '61
☐ G-ASUG	Beech D.18S	US '56
☐ G-ATFG	Brantly B.2B	US '65
☐ G-ATOY	Piper Comanche 260B	US '65
☐ G-AXEH	SAL Bulldog Srs 1	'69
☐ G-BBVF	SAL Twin Pioneer 2	'58
☐ G-BDFU	Dragonfly man-powered aircraft	'75
☐ G-BDIX	DH Comet 4C	'62
☐ VH-SNB	DH Dragon I	'34
☐ VH-UQB	DH Puss Moth	§ '34
☐ W-2	Weir W-2 autogyro (BAPC.85)	'34
☐ TE462	Supermarine Spitfire XVI	'45
☐ 'TJ398'	Auster AOP.6 (BAPC.70)	'44
☐ VM360	Avro Anson C.19 (G-APHV)	'47
☐ WF259	Hawker Sea Hawk F.2 [171-A]	'54
☐ WV493	Percival Provost T.1 (G-BDYG) [29]	'53
☐ WW145	DH Sea Venom FAW.22 [680-LM]	'55

☐ XA109	DH Sea Vampire T.22	§ '54
☐ XG594	Westland Whirlwind HAS.7 [517-PO]	US '57
☐ XL762	SARO Skeeter AOP.12	'58
☐ XM597	Avro Vulcan B.2	'63
☐ XN776	EE Lightning F.2A [C]	'62
☐ XT288	HS Buccaneer S.2B	'66
☐ 309	MiG-15UTI 'Midget'	Ru c55
☐ 591	Schleicher Rhonlerche II	Gr c60
☐ 3677	MiG MiG-15bis 'Fagot'	Ru c53
☐ 9940	Bristol Bolingbroke IVT	'44
☐ 191659	Messerschmitt Me 163B-1a [15]	Gr '45
☐ –	Chargus 18/50 hang glider (BAPC.160)	c75
☐	Cirrus 3 hang glider (BAPC.197)	c75
☐ –	Mignet HM.14 Flying Flea (BAPC.12)	Fr '36
☐ –	Moonraker 77 hang glider (BAPC.195)	c77
☐ –	MS.505 Criquet (G-BIRW) [FI+S]	Gr '47
☐ –	Pilcher Hawk (BAPC.49)	1896
☐	Sigma IIM hang glider (BAPC.196)	c80
☐ –	Slingsby Tutor/glider (BCB)	'45
☐ –	Slingsby Gull I glider (BED)	c46
☐ –	Slingsby T.21B glider (BJV)	c60
☐ –	WACO CG-4A Hadrian nose	US '44

ALSO IN SCOTLAND

The **MONTROSE AERODROME MUSEUM SOCIETY** are hard at work establishing a museum on the site of the former airfield which holds arguably the oldest buildings designed for military flying extant in the United Kingdom. Work is in its early stages at present but visitors are welcome by prior arrangement. Contact: Montrose Aerodrome Museum Society, 96 Market Street, Brechin, Angus, Scotland, D9 6BD.

The start of a museum, Whirlwind HAR.10 XJ723 and Vampire T.11 XE874 (despite the personality clash on the booms!) Otger van der Kooij

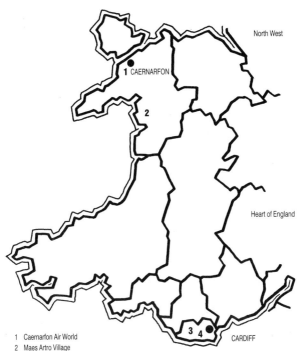

WALES

North West

1 CAERNARFON

2

Heart of England

3 4 CARDIFF

1 Caernarfon Air World
2 Maes Artro Village
3 Wales Aircraft Museum
4 Welsh Industrial & Maritime
  Museum

Wales Tourist Board
Brunel House, 2 Fitzalan Road, Cardiff, CF2 1UY
Tel: 01222 499909 Fax: 01222 485031

CAERNARFON AIR WORLD
Caernarfon Aerodrome, Gwynedd

Address: Snowdon Mountain Aviation, Caernarfon Airport, Llandwrog, Caernarfon, Gwynedd, LL54 5TP.

Telephone: 01286 830800, Fax 01286 830280.

Where: At Caernarfon aerodrome, north of the A487 and signposted from Llandwrog.

Open: March 1 to November 30, 9.30am to 5.30pm. Groups at other times can be arranged.

By bus: Services pass close by, enquiries via museum.

By rail: Bangor 12 miles.

Tourist: Caernarfon 01267 231557.

Admission: Adult £3.50, Child £2.50.

Facilities: Toilets/Parking/Cafe/Shop/Disabled/Kids/All/Changes/Brochure.

Situated within sight of the Snowdon mountain range, the museum naturally includes themes relating to mountain rescue and to mountain crashes. The history of RAF Llandwrog is well illustrated. Visitors can see the restoration of the Anson underway at weekends. Pleasure flying is run during the summer season from the aerodrome, often using the Air Atlantique DH Dragon Rapide G-AIDL. Views of the activity on the aerodrome can be seen to advantage from the museum.

Aircraft exhibits:

☐ G-ALFT	DH Dove 6		'49
☐ G-AMLZ	Percival Prince 6E		'51
☐ TX235	Avro Anson C.19/2		'46
☐ WM961	Hawker Sea Hawk FB.5 [J]		'54
☐ WN499	Westland Dragonfly HR.3 [Y]	US	'53
☐ WV781	Bristol Sycamore HR.12		'52
☐ XA282	Slingsby Cadet TX.3		'52
☐ XD599	DH Vampire T.11 [A]		'54
☐ XH837	Gloster Javelin FAW.7 nose		'58
☐ XJ726	Westland Whirlwind HAR.10 [F]	US	'55
☐ XK623	DH Vampire T.11 [56]		'56
☐ –	Mignet HM.14 Flying Flea (BAPC 201)	Fr	'36

Nearby:
Bangor and the Menai Bridge, *12 miles.*
Caernarfon, *4 miles.*
Ffestiniog Railway, *16 miles.*
Llanberis Lake Railway, *8 miles.*
Portmeirion Village, *16 miles.*
Snowdon Mountain Railway, *10 miles.*

Clever use of mural and the salvaged 'tail feathers' of an Anson to show a high ground incident. Ken Ellis

Above: **Dragon Rapide G-AIDL is often used for pleasure flights from Caernarfon.** Alan Curry
Below: **Cadet TX3 glider 'flies' from the aircraft hall roof.** Nigel Price

MAES ARTRO VILLAGE
Llanbedr, Gwynedd

Address: Artro Enterprises, Reception Building, Maes Artro, Llanbedr, Gwynedd, LL45 2PZ.
Telephone: 01341 241467.
Where: In Llanbedr village, south of Harlech on the A496.
Open: Daily Easter to the end of September 10am to 5.30pm.
By bus: Services to Barmouth and Harlech pass close to the entrance.
By rail: Llanbedr Halt on the Cambrian Coast line, half mile.
Tourist: Barmouth* 01654 761244.
Admission: Adult £2.95, OAP £2.45, Child £2.25.
Facilities: Toilets/Parking/Cafe/Shop/Disabled/ Kids/All/Brochure.

Part of the former domestic site for the nearby airfield has been turned into an attractive visitor centre appealing to everyone. From an aviation viewpoint, the history of Llanbedr airfield and its surroundings are well covered and work on the restoration of the Anson – a long time resident at the airfield – is possible during weekends. Also included on the site is a recreated old Welsh-style street, rural heritage exhibition, sea life aquarium, woodland walk and much more.

Aircraft exhibits:

☐	'MW467'	V-S Spitfire V replica (BAPC.202)	'45
☐	VS562	Avro Anson T.21	'48
☐	XJ409	Westland Whirlwind HAR.10	US '53
☐	–	Hawker Hunter cockpit	c55
☐	A92-664	GAF Jindivik 4A drone	Aus c57

Nearby:

Fairbourne Railway, 8 miles.
Ffestiniog Railway, 10 miles.
Portmeirion Village, 10 miles.
Shell Island – offering good views of activity at the Test & Experimental Establishment Llanbedr, 2 miles.

Above: **Visitors can see work underway on the Maes Artro Anson.** Ken Ellis
Below: **The aircraft was the protoype T.21 and made its first flight in 1948.** Authors collection

Dassault Mystère IVA at the Wales Aircraft Museum.
John Uncles

WALES AIRCRAFT MUSEUM

Cardiff-Wales Airport, South Glamorgan

Address: D R Sims, 19 Castle Road, Rhoose, near Barry, South Glamorgan, CF6 9EU.
Telephone: 01446 711141.
Where: At Cardiff-Wales Airport, near Barry, signposted off the M4.
Open: 10am to 6pm every day May to September and weekends 1pm to 4.30pm the remainder of the year.
By bus: Services to the Airport from Barry and Cardiff.
By rail: Barry Island 4 miles.
Tourist: Cardiff 01222 499909, Fax 01222 485031.
Admission: Adult £2, Child £1.
Facilities: Toilets/Parking/Cafe/Shop/Disabled/Kids/All/Changes.

Located on the edge of Cardiff-Wales Airport and affording views of the activity there, the Wales Aircraft Museum has an aircraft display park containing a wide variety of post-war military aircraft and a Vickers Viscount airliner, once a common site at the airport.

Aircraft exhibits:

☐ G-AOJC	Vickers Viscount 802	'56
☐ WJ576	EE Canberra T.17	'53
☐ WM292	Gloster Meteor TT.20 [841]	'53
☐ WP515	EE Canberra B.2 nose	'52
☐ WV826	Hawker Sea Hawk FGA.6 [147-Z]	'54
☐ 'XF383'	Hawker Hunter F.51 (E-409)	'56
☐ XG883	Fairey Gannet T.5 [773]	'57
☐ XL449	Fairey Gannet AEW.3	'58
☐ XM569	Avro Vulcan B.2	'63
☐ XN458	Hunting Jet Provost T.3 [19]	'60
☐ XN650	DH Sea Vixen FAW.2	'61
☐ XN928	Blackburn Buccaneer S.1 [353]	'62
☐ XT911	McDD Phantom FGR.2 nose	'69
☐ ZF578	EE Lightning F.53	'67
☐ 'NZ233'	Vickers Varsity T.1 (WJ944)	'53
☐ 59	Dassault Mystère IVA [2-SF]	Fr '55
☐ 29963	Lockheed T-33A 'T-Bird'	US '52
☐ '63000'	NA F-100D Super Sabre (42160) [FW-000]	US '54

Nearby:

City of Cardiff, *10 miles*.
Newport Transporter Bridge, *16 miles*.
Welsh Industrial and Maritime Museum, *10 miles*
– see page 120.   See overleaf.

Above: **Hawker Sea Hawk FGA.6 sporting Suez campaign stripes at the Wales Aircraft Museum.** John Uncles

WELSH INDUSTRIAL & MARITIME MUSEUM

Cardiff Docks, South Glamorgan.

Address: Bute Street, Cardiff, CF1 6AN.
Telephone: 01222 481919.
Where: In Cardiff Docks, well signposted from the city centre.
Open: Daily except Monday (Bank Holidays excepted) Tuesday to Saturday 10am to 5pm and Sundays 2.30pm to 5pm.
By bus: Services serve close by, enquire with the museum.
By rail: Cardiff central 2 miles.
Tourist: Cardiff 01222 499909, Fax 01222 485031.
Admission: Adult £1.50, OAP/cons £1.15, Children 75p.
Facilities: Toilets/Parking/Cafe/Shop/Disabled/All/X.

Set in the heart of Cardiff's dockland, the museum serves to illustrate Welsh marine and industrial achievements. Within the site a Westland Wessex helicopter provides an aviation theme.

Aircraft exhibit:

☐ XM300	Westland Wessex HAS.1	US '59

Nearby:
City of Cardiff centre, *2 miles.*
Newport Transporter Bridge, *8 miles.*
Wales Aircraft Museum, *10 miles – see page 119.*

NORTHERN IRELAND

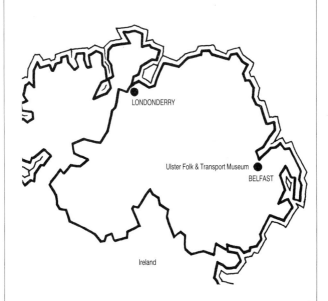

Northern Ireland Tourist Board
St Anne's Court, 59 North Street, Belfast, BT1 1NB
Tel: 01232 231221 Fax: 01232 240960

ULSTER FOLK AND TRANSPORT MUSEUM

Holywood, County Down

Address: Cultra Manor, Holywood, Northern Ireland, BT18 0EU.
Telephone: 01232 421444, Fax 02132 428728.
Where: On the A2 north east of Belfast city centre at Holywood. Well signed.
Open: Open daily all year round, closed three days at Xmas. July-August Monday to Saturday 10.30am to 6pm, Sunday 12am to 6pm; April-June and September Monday-Friday 9.30am to 5pm, Saturday 10.30am to 6pm, Sunday 12am to 6pm; October to March Monday to Friday 9.30am to 4pm and Saturday-Sunday 12.30am to 4.30pm.
By bus: Services from Belfast to Holywood and beyond pass the entrance.
By rail: Holywood 2 miles.
Tourist: 01232 231221, Fax 01232 240960.
Admission: Adult £3.30, OAP/Child £2.20, Family ticket £8.
Facilities: Toilets/Parking/Cafe/Shop/Disabled/All/Changes/Brochure.

The transport element of this extensive museum has prospered in recent years with the opening in 1994 of an amazing railway hall and a land transport hall in 1995. It is hoped that more space can then be devoted to aviation as the Province has a rich heritage to show off. Currently the 'original' Ferguson replica and the Short SC.1 are used to show the full sweep of aviation development. In a superb display devoted to the life and works of Rex McCandless, two of his autogyros are displayed as well as his legendary motorcycles and the four-wheel drive 'buggy'. Across the road on the 'Folk' site can be found an incredible village of buildings moved and reconstructed, brick-by-brick from sites all over Northern Ireland. Regular special displays and exhibitions and other attractions, details on application.

Aircraft exhibits:

☐	G-AJOC	Miles Messenger 2A	§ '47
☐	G-AKEL	Miles Gemini 1A	§ '47
☐	G-AKGE	Miles Gemini 3C	§ '47
☐	G-AKLW	Short Sealand	§ '51
☐	G-AOUR	DH Tiger Moth	§ '44
☐	G-ARTZ	McCandless M-2 gyroplane	'65
☐	G-ATXX	McCandless M-4 gyroplane	'66
☐	VH-UUP	Short Scion I	§ '34
☐	XG905	Short SC.1	'58
☐	–	Ferguson Monoplane replica (IAHC.6)	'09
☐	–	Ferguson Monoplane replica (IAHC.9)	§ '09
☐	–	Short Nimbus I glider (ALA)	§ '47

Nearby:

City of Belfast, 7 miles.
North Down Heritage Centre, Bangor, 12 miles.
Ulster Aviation Society, 20 miles – see below.

ALSO IN NORTHERN IRELAND

At Langford Lodge aerodrome, west of Crumlin, the **ULSTER AVIATION SOCIETY** have established their extensive collection of aircraft and artefacts. Included in the collection are Shorts 330 G-BDBS and Grumman Wildcat V JV482. The aerodrome – within the beautiful Lough Neagh Wildlife Sanctuary – has an interesting past and the Society have started restoration of its probably unique control tower. Plans are to open on a regular basis each Saturday, but as 'Aviation Museums of Britain' went to press, these plans could not be confirmed. Until this time, visits can be made by prior arrangement. Contact: Ray Burrows, 49 Circular Road, Belfast, BT4 2GA and enclose an SAE.

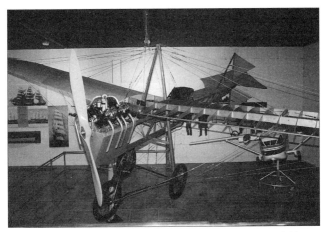

Above: Within the Ulster Folk and Transport Museum can be found a faithful replica of the monoplane built by Ulsterman Harry Ferguson – he later gained considerable fame for his tractors and ploughing system.

Below: Largest exhibit with the Ulster Aviation Society is the second prototype Shorts 330 commuter liner, first flown at Belfast on 8th July 1975. Both Ken Ellis

IRELAND

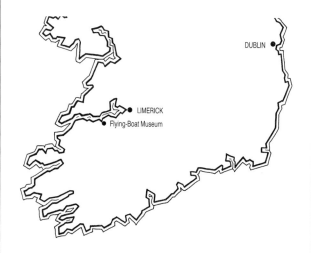

Northern Ireland

DUBLIN ●

● LIMERICK
● Flying-Boat Museum

Irish Tourist Board
150 New Bond Street, London, W1Y 0AQ
Tel: 0171 493 3201 Fax: 0171 493 9065

FLYING-BOAT MUSEUM

Foynes, Limerick

Address: Flying-Boat Museum, Foynes, Limerick.
Telephone: 00 353 69 65416 (also Fax).
Where: On the N69 west of Limerick, well signed.
Open: Open March 31 to November 1, 10am to 6pm.
By bus: Daily service from Limerick.
By rail: Limerick 23 miles.
Admission: Adult £3, Child £1.50, Family £8.
Facilities: Toilets/Parking/Cafe/Shop/Disabled/ All/Brochure.

From 1939 to 1945 Foynes was famous as the only place from which non-stop services to and from the USA could be made. The museum is centred around the original terminal building, control tower, radio and weather rooms of the famous flying-boat station. The museum records the magnificent era of the flying-boat and Ireland's vital role to the Allied war effort during the Second World War. Foynes was where Irish Coffee was invented and visitors can sample this and other Irish welcomes!

The remains of BOAC Sunderland III G-AGES are among the artefacts held at Foynes. Here fellow G-AGJO of 1948 provides the flavour of a great era. Author's collection

INDEX

As well as listing county names, this index has been extended to list some museums also by 'alternative' or 'generic' names to aid reference.

We hope that you have enjoyed this Midland Publishing book. Our titles are carefully edited and designed for you by a knowledgeable and enthusiastic team of specialists, with over 20 years experience. Further titles are in the course of preparation but we would welcome ideas on what you would like to see. If you have a manuscript or project that requires publishing, we should be happy to consider it; brief details initially, please.

In addition, our associate company, Midland Counties Publications, offer an exceptionally wide range of aviation and railway books/videos for sale by mail-order around the world. For a copy of the appropriate catalogue, please write, telephone or fax to:

Midland Counties Publications
Unit 3 Maizefield, Hinckley Fields, Hinckley, Leics, LE10 1YF.
Tel: 01455 233 747; Fax: 01455 841 805.

Also in the series . . .

**BRITISH AIRFIELD BUILDINGS
OF THE SECOND WORLD WAR**
Pocket Guide No 1
Graham Buchan Innes

The world of airfield buildings is one
of constant fascination to enthusiasts. Until now, references on this
subject have been the domain of
vary specialist works, or to be
partially found within high price
books. All of this has conspired to
put off a whole army of people who
have a thirst for such knowledge.
British Airfield Buildings is the
answer to this need and in a
genuinely pocket-sized form. From
control towers, to hangars, to
defensive strongpoints, barrack
blocks, maintenance buildings, to
the humble latrine, it provides an
illustration of a *surviving* example,
highlighting details and other styles
of similar buildings.

Over 200 illustrations with brief but
informative captions take the reader
for an excursion through a typical
wartime station. *British Airfield
Buildings* provides an ideal primer to
a subject close to the heart of all
enthusiasts.

Softback, 148 x 105mm, 128 pages,
230 photographs
ISBN 1 85780 026 5
£5.95

Available from
Midland Counties Publications
Unit 3 Maizefield, Hinckley Fields, Hinckley, Leics, LE10 1YF
Tel: 01455 233 747   Fax: 01455 841 805